THE STRUCTURE OF
CHRISTIAN EXISTENCE

THE SEABURY LIBRARY OF CONTEMPORARY THEOLOGY

THE
STRUCTURE
OF
CHRISTIAN
EXISTENCE

John B. Cobb, Jr.

A Crossroad Book
The Seabury Press • New York

1979
The Seabury Press
815 Second Avenue
New York, N.Y. 10017

Published 1967 by The Westminster Press
Seabury paperback edition 1979

Library of Congress Catalog Card Number: 78-68576
ISBN: 0-8164-2229-X

Printed in the United States of America

CONTENTS

PREFACE

THIS BOOK IS AN INQUIRY into what is distinctive in Christianity and into its claim to finality. Christianity is viewed primarily as one structure of existence among other such structures. The emergence of each structure is a historical phenomenon closely correlated in most instances with particular beliefs.

The outcome of this inquiry has sweeping implications for a number of questions. Some of its implications for the world mission of Christianity are apparent. Its implications for the self-understanding of the church and its ministry are important, although somewhat less clear. Equally important are the implications for understanding the relation between cognitive beliefs and the several structures of existence. If the conclusions of the study are accepted, the understanding of the nature and function of the theological enterprise as a whole will be affected. In these and other ways the book constitutes critical conversation with other current theologies.

However, it has seemed best to omit discussion of these implications. Brief treatment would add little, and adequate treatment would require great expansion of the book. Similarly, I have omitted polemics and have not even attempted to explain the similarities and differences of my position in comparison with those of other theologians. Such discussion also would have greatly complicated the exposition and expanded the size of the book. I hope in the future to have opportunities to develop some of the implications and to engage in discussion and debate on relevant points with my colleagues.

During most of the preparation of this book, it was my intention to include an explicit treatment of Christology. That the content is relevant to this doctrine will, I hope, be apparent. But, in addition to the historical work of Jesus, Christology must deal with his "person" in terms of the mode of God's presence in him. This requires, on the one hand, the use of philosophical categories such as those I developed in *A Christian Natural Theology* and, on the other hand, reflection on the relation of the way God was present in Jesus to the way he is present elsewhere. It must deal also with the relation of claims about God's efficacy in history to the work of the historian. Inclusion of such issues would have unduly extended the argument. Some indication of my views on these questions can be found in my essays on "The Finality of Christ in a Whiteheadian Perspective"[1] and "Ontology, History, and Christian Faith."[2] A Christology along these lines is my next major project.

Methodologically, the content of the present book has much in common with Christian natural theology as that is characterized in my earlier book. That is, it bears the clear imprint of my Christian perspective in its perception, selection, and organization of the material. At the same time, it seeks to be faithful to the material and to avoid special pleading or any normative appeal to what Christians believe. Nevertheless, it would stretch the meaning of "natural theology" too far to include this kind of historical analysis within it. I conceive natural theology as the area of overlap between philosophy and theology, whereas this book deals chiefly with the area of overlap between history and theology. Natural theology, while it need not be naturalistic, looks for its primary data to nature — to what is universal, recurrent, or widespread — rather than to the specifics of history.

[1] This was prepared as a lecture for the Third Oxford Institute on Methodist Theological Studies held in July, 1965. Dr. Dow Kirkpatrick, the leader of the American delegation, has edited a volume, *The Finality of Christ* (Abingdon Press, 1966), containing all the lectures delivered at that conference. There is some overlapping of the discussion of finality in Chapter Twelve of this book with the content of the first section of that lecture. I am grateful for Abingdon's permission to include in this book several paragraphs (see n. 25) that are almost identical with paragraphs in the earlier essay. In other respects my views on Christology have changed slightly since the time this lecture was given.

[2] *Religion in Life*, Spring, 1965.

Despite the many limitations I have imposed on the book, the project remains an ambitious one, and I am painfully aware that my historical knowledge is not adequate to it. That I have decided, nevertheless, to pursue the task and to make public the judgments to which I have come is an expression of my conviction that this approach to the understanding of Christian faith is a needed supplement and corrective to those approaches that are currently dominant. It is my hope that the numerous inadequacies (and perhaps also inaccuracies) of the exposition will not prevent the book from contributing a useful perspective on some of the critical problems of Christian theology.

I have used very little documentation. This is because much of the material could be derived from many sources, whereas most of the concepts that have determined the way this material is used are my own. Where I have directly borrowed from one source, or am conscious of special indebtedness, I have given the reference. This kind of indebtedness applies especially to Susanne Langer, *Philosophy in a New Key,* and Heinrich Zimmer, *Philosophies of India,* on which I have leaned heavily for portions of Chapters Three and Six respectively. Also, the understanding of Gnosticism reflected in the Appendix is largely dependent on Hans Jonas, *The Gnostic Religion.*

I want to make acknowledgment of another sort to those books which have been landmarks in my thought on topics dealt with here, even when in the end their influence on what is said may be only indirect. The five books that now seem to me to have been most important in this way are Reinhold Niebuhr, *The Self and the Dramas of History;* Mircea Eliade, *The Myth of the Eternal Return;* Erich Neumann, *The Origins and History of Consciousness;* Rudolf Bultmann, *Primitive Christianity in Its Contemporary Setting;* and Karl Jaspers, *The Origin and Goal of History.* I am conscious of a lesser indebtedness to Gilbert Murray, *The Five Stages of Greek Religion;* F. M. Cornford, *From Religion to Philosophy;* Lewis Mumford, *The Transformations of Man;* Jean-Paul Sartre, *Being and Nothingness;* Michael Polanyi, *The Study of Man;* H. P. van Dusen, *Spirit, Son and Father;* Anders Nygren, *Agape and Eros;* Edward Bullough, *Aesthetics;* Thorleif Boman, *Hebrew Thought Compared with Greek;* and additional books by Bultmann. Such a list could be indefinitely expanded but with diminishing significance. The influence of Whitehead's philosophy is so pervasive on my thought that the book as a whole might be called a Whiteheadian doctrine of man. But Whitehead himself gave serious attention to but few of the topics discussed.

The questions with which this book chiefly deals first began to claim major attention from me through my participation in the Institute of Liberal Arts at Emory University and especially in the seminars on classical Greece. I am indebted to several colleagues for stimulation, but I want to single out Prof. Robert Scranton, now of the University of Chicago, for special mention. Since coming to Claremont in 1958, I have had the opportunity to work out my ideas from time to time in courses on the nature of man. Actual work toward the book began in such a class in the Spring Semester of 1965. I am indebted to all the students who have encouraged me by their interest, but especially to those on whom I inflicted the reading of some of the early manuscript material.

During the year 1965–1966, much of this material was included in somewhat different form in my lectures as Fulbright Visiting Professor at the Johannes Gutenberg University in Mainz, Germany. In April and May I gave the first series of Jaspers Lectures at Ripon Hall, near Oxford, England. Portions of the material here offered were included in these lectures on " The Finality of Jesus and Jaspers' Doctrine of the Axial Period." Weekly during the summer session at Mainz, I met informally with a group of instructors and advanced students. Much of the content of this book was discussed at those sessions. I would like to take this opportunity to express my appreciation to the Protestant theological faculty at Mainz, as well as to the Fulbright Commission and particularly to Prof. Wolfhart Pannenberg for making the year at Mainz both possible and enjoyable; to the Jaspers Lectureship Committee, the students at Ripon Hall, and especially to Principal W. G. Fallows for an experience I shall always remember with special pleasure; and to the members of the discussion group at Mainz and particularly its leader Dr. Traugott Koch for the sharp but always generous criticisms I received.

Among my colleagues, Professors Donald Rhoades, Wolfhart

Pannenberg, and Hans Dieter Betz have read the manuscript in a late stage of its writing. All have helped me to improve it and have also made me more clearly aware than ever how much more improvement is really needed. My student assistant, Mr. David Griffin, has been tireless and perceptive both in criticism of details and in calling attention to weaknesses in organization and lack of clarity in the argument. The Index is his work. Mr. Dalton Baldwin also made some helpful criticisms.

During the entire period in which I have been seriously reflecting on these questions, the greatest personal influence on my thought has been Prof. Thomas Altizer. The character of this influence is difficult to describe, since the great difference in our views as well as in our temperament will be apparent to even the casual reader. But again and again I have been jolted out of habits of mind too easily fallen into and have had new vistas opened before me by his criticisms, his suggestions, and his original work. Altizer also read the entire manuscript in a late version and made many penetrating and valuable comments. I have taken some of them into account and wish that I could have coped more adequately with others.

In conclusion I want to express my gratitude to Dr. E. C. " Pomp " Colwell, with whose work my professional life has been closely related for twenty years at Chicago, at Emory, and in Claremont. Wherever he goes, he creates a climate of mutual respect, freedom of thought, and encouragement of study and writing, from which I have benefited greatly. This book is dedicated to him.

J. B. C., Jr.

School of Theology at Claremont
Claremont, California

Chapter One

INTRODUCTION

CHRISTIANS HAVE ALWAYS lived with the awareness that there are other communities in the world with other ways of believing and acting. Through most of Christian history, Christians have assumed that the relation to these other communities is one of difference and of fulfillment to promise, of better to worse, or of truth to error. As long as the origin and uniqueness of Christianity were understood supernaturalistically, such a view was inevitable. Since the breakdown of supernaturalism, the claims of Christianity to uniqueness and to finality have continued, but they have required justification.

Thus far, the major efforts to understand the distinctiveness and the finality of Christianity have been those made in that great movement of Christian thought in Germany, which we call nineteenth-century theology. Hegel, Schleiermacher, and Troeltsch represent its highest achievements with respect to our present concerns. Nevertheless, they provide us relatively little help today. Hegel and Schleiermacher did not sense the full seriousness of the claims of other religions, especially those of India, to rival and replace Christianity, and they treated them instead as stages in a single line of progress leading to Christianity. Although Troeltsch saw in his *Die Absolutheit des Christentums* (1901) that one could not treat these religions in this hierarchical way, he also so described the religions of India as to imply a clear inferiority. Later he realized that, on the one hand, he had done them a serious injustice, and that, on the other hand, every form of Christianity is no less closely bound to the particularities of culture than are these other religions. Thereupon, in his limitless openness and honesty, he retreated from his earlier claims and affirmed fundamental equality of the several higher religions, regarding each as indissolubly bound to its own culture.[3] By that time the powerful Barthian proclamation was turning the energies of the theologians away from the question, empirically, historically, and philosophically formulated, as to the uniqueness and finality of Christianity. Today, with the decline of neo-orthodoxy, the question arises again with even greater force and urgency.

Two other criticisms must be directed against the nineteenth-century quest in addition to that of its self-acknowledged failure. First, the question of the distinctive essence of Christianity was subordinated to that of its superiority to other religions in such a way that the former question was inadequately treated. To determine the distinctive essence of Christianity, we should hold initially in abeyance the question of its relative value or excellence. Only when each religion is understood in its own uniqueness can questions of relative value be honestly treated.

Second, all three men closely identified religion with God's mode of presence in history, and all three saw their task as that of comparing Christianity with other religions. But Troeltsch's assumption that "we cannot live without religion"[4] is no longer ours. The importance of religion is just as problematic for us as the importance of Christianity. We must understand Christianity in relation to the several forms of secularism just as much as in relation to world religions. Furthermore, in considering what we are accustomed to call religions, we have come to recognize that "God" may not be involved at all. The choice between theism and atheism is a different choice from that between religion and secularism. In this situation, the problem of understanding the distinctiveness of Christianity must be approached quite differently.

One approach, not infrequently adopted, is in the realm of ideas. Every competitor with Christianity for man's loyalty assumes the form of a system of beliefs, positive and negative. We can compare Christian beliefs about man, the world, God, origin, and destiny with

    [3] Ernst Troeltsch, *Christian Thought: Its History and Application* (Meridian Books, Inc., 1957), pp. 51–52.
    [4] *Ibid.*, p. 25.

those of scientific humanism and Marxism as well as with those of Buddhism and Confucianism. This is undoubtedly important and valid. If beliefs essential to a position are false, or if in comparison with other beliefs they are exposed as clearly inadequate, then the position as such is rendered impossible, whatever advantages it may seem otherwise to have.

Nevertheless, the study of comparative doctrine will not take us far. In the first place, the diversity of beliefs among Christians is vast, and when we ask theologians to tell us which of these beliefs are of supreme importance, the diversity is not decreased. Beliefs that some regard as essential others hold to be incredible. In other religions a similar diversity is to be found. In a comparative study of beliefs, one is ultimately reduced to comparing individual spokesmen for the several movements.

In the second place, most Christians agree that what is essentially important lies deeper than assent to doctrine. The relation of intellectual assent to these other dimensions of Christianity is not one of perfect correlation. Few would claim that right belief guarantees a loving relation to one's neighbor or that all persons who err in their beliefs are inferior in love. The accurate formulation of the relation of beliefs to more ultimate aspects of Christianity will be possible only when we treat these more ultimate aspects directly and see how they are, in fact, informed by beliefs.

In the third place, some Christian doctrines in most formulations refer to real changes effected in real people. This segment of Christian belief can only be discussed in relation to what has, in fact, taken place. It can be argued that the truth and validity of ideas are in no way measured by their results, but few of us would remain Christian today if we were convinced that the consequences of Christian belief were consistently destructive of personality and society.

For these and other reasons (including the fact that I have dealt and intend further to deal with problems of belief in other contexts), I propose that we reject both religion and ideas as the primary context or vehicle for the investigation of the distinctive essence of Christianity and employ, instead, the category of " structures of existence." It is my conviction that Christianity brought into being a structure of existence different from those of Judaism and of Greek humanism as well as from that of such Eastern religions as Buddhism. It is my project in this book to show that this is so and to describe this distinctive structure of existence in its relation to the others.

To claim that Christianity embodies a distinctive structure of existence does not involve the claim that this structure of existence is better or worse than other structures. I am convinced there is real diversity in the world — that Buddhist existence is profoundly different from Socratic existence, and that prophetic existence is different from both. The claim that Christian existence also is different from all the others is a denial that it is simply a subdivision of one of them, such as the prophetic, and it affirms the importance of choosing between Christianity and other alternatives. The last chapter deals with the comparison and relative valuation of the several structures of existence, but this is preceded by an attempt to understand each structure as a peculiar and, in its own terms, ideal embodiment of human possibility. The question of comparative value cannot be appropriately treated until the radicality of the diversity is fully recognized.

The meaning of the expression "structure of existence," which plays such an important role in this entire approach, will hopefully become progressively clearer to the reader as he proceeds. However, some advance explanation is needed. The term "existence" is taken from existentialism, although in part the treatment here will differ. "Existence" refers to what a subject is in and for himself in his givenness to himself. But attention should not be concentrated exclusively on consciousness. Indeed, the interplay of conscious and unconscious elements within existence is one important factor differentiating the several structures of existence.

Existentialists seem typically to assume that the possibilities for man, the possible structures of existence, are and have always been fixed. They analyze with great sensitivity the different modes of existence that are chosen, especially in man's innumerable attempts to evade a full and responsible acceptance of his situation. But they appear to think that just this range of modes of existence is that within which man as man has always operated.

Insofar as this is implied, I disagree. The existentialists are describing the several modes of existence among which modern man chooses, but the possibility of choosing among just these modes is itself the product of a history. The range of modes of existence available to primitive man, for example, was different. To designate this more radical kind of difference, I use the phrase " structure of existence."

The conviction that there is a diversity of structures of existence as well as a diversity of modes of existence within each structure is partly a function of reflection on human differences and partly a function of a priori considerations. The validity of the results of the reflection can be supported only by the book as a whole, but the structure of the book and of the argument can only be understood in the light of the a priori considerations as well.

The assumption is that man has really evolved from subhuman animal forms. His evolution involved the subjective side of life as well as the objective; that is, negatively, we are not to think of great inexplicable gaps in the forms of subjective existence any more than in the forms of biological organisms. It is quite incredible that the structure of existence described by Heidegger in *Being and Time* appeared suddenly in the world, directly superseding an apelike existence. If the evidence required us to assume that the earliest beings we call human did in fact embody this structure of existence, then we would have to posit exceedingly high levels of mentality in our prehuman ancestors, assuming that for hundreds of thousands of years they must have *far* more closely approximated our contemporary existence than does any now existing nonhuman member of the simian family.

However, such evidence as we have points in a quite different direction. It seems highly probable that as recently as ten thousand years ago the structure of man's existence was still quite different from ours. Hence, it can be assumed that after biological evolution had long ceased to have importance, new structures of existence continued to develop in man.

The purpose of this book is to identify and appraise that structure of existence which came into being in and with Christianity. To understand such a phenomenon and to gain the perspective necessary for its appraisal, we must understand how it arose and how it has been related to other such phenomena. Hence, an evolutionary-historical approach is required. This does not mean that the later is necessarily superior to the earlier, or that historical triumph guarantees truth or rightness. But it does mean that understanding of the way in which one movement arises out of another and interacts with others is an important factor in determining responsible judgments about it.[5]

The bulk of this book is an attempt to describe the emergence of new structures of existence, including the Christian one. Such an attempt is possible only by a process of highly selective generalization, simplification, and abstraction. My hope in offering the book is that the abstractions will prove fruitful beyond their particular application here.

The necessity for abstraction and simplification is readily apparent. In my view, only individuals are actual, and for our purposes that means that the final real entities with which we are dealing are momentary embodiments of human existence. These are virtually infinite in number, and no two have ever been quite alike. To speak usefully of modes of existence, however, we cannot refer to these endless variations. We must group them together in types or classes. But to do so means to impose an order upon them, and the type of order imposed depends upon the categories employed.

For example, one can classify such moments of existence according to their emotional content, and then one must make the further choice as to what classification of emotions he will employ. Or he can classify according to the ways in which reason and emotion interact, or the ways in which one entity takes account of other entities, or the extent to which it is self-determining. No one classification is true or false — only better or worse for certain purposes.

I am, furthermore, making a distinction between modes of existence and structures of existence. This distinction, too, is a simplification. No sharp line can be drawn between diversities of mode and diversities of structure. The choice of modes within a structure affects in time the structure as well. Furthermore, the greater inclusiveness of a structure is purchased at the price of still greater abstractness.

---

[5] Readers impatient with methodological and other preliminary considerations may wish to proceed directly to Chapter Three. However, they should not expect a full understanding of all the categories there employed.

Because of this element of arbitrariness, it is important to make my assumptions explicit. These are that the major religions and cultures of mankind embody different structures of existence, and that this is the deepest and most illuminating way to view their differences. If this is correct, then the distinctive essence of Christianity can best be seen in terms of the structure of Christian existence, and it can best be compared with other claimants for our allegiance at this level.

Two additional methodological questions should be mentioned. First, in describing a structure of existence, one must distinguish between the self-understanding of those who participate in it and our understanding of it. The latter plays the primary role in this book. However, our understanding must be derived from investigation of the self-understanding and must illumine it. Also, the development of the structures themselves was dependent on particular self-understandings. Especially when the self-understanding was a reflective one, any understanding on our part should take it with utmost seriousness as we attempt to describe the structure of existence that it brings to expression.

Second, there is an acute terminological problem that is complicated by the interconnection of self-understanding and present explanation. To compare the several structures of existence with each other, it is necessary to employ terms foreign to the self-understanding of some of them and even to use terms employed by them in ways not identical with their own usage. This would not be so problematic were it not for the fact that these terms also lack clear definition in our normal modern usage. Hence, in some instances terms are used in ways, hopefully made clear in the contexts, that are alien to the self-understanding of those to whom they are applied and also highly specialized in relation to ordinary usage today.

For example, the idea of " a person " is, on the one hand, strange to the Old Testament and, on the other hand, often indistinguishable today from that of " a human being." Despite this fact, I have employed it to refer to a particular kind of existence that emerged for the first time in Israel. The justification is that no other word seems better to designate this structure of existence and that those aspects of humanness, which are especially brought into focus for us by the idea of personhood, received their decisive embodiment first in Israel. In other senses, of course, primitives, Indians, and Greeks were " persons," too. The situation is similar with respect to my treatment of " mythical," " reflective," " rational," " reason," " will," " responsibility," " the sense of ought," "self-transcendence," " spirit," and many other terms.

In the development of our present-day structure of existence out of those of prehuman animal existence, there were no drastic discontinuities. On the other hand, this book attempts to define clearly differentiated structures, some of which have succeeded others. Such succession implies discontinuity. But there need be no contradiction between the affirmations of continuity and discontinuity, and indeed both are affirmed in any intelligent theory of evolution or development. This can be easily shown.

One of the major obstacles to early acceptance of evolutionary theory in biology was the empirical fact of relatively fixed species. The discovery that there were far more species than originally supposed and that these shaded off into one another helped to overcome this objection. Nevertheless, biologists still think in terms of species and differentiate between the range of variety to be found within a given species and the differences that distinguish one species from another. This differentiation is not absolute, and it has arbitrary elements in its application, but it points to the fact that, through a process of gradual change, forms emerge which constitute something new, and which then have the capacity to perpetuate themselves indefinitely.

The process of the development of new structures of existence shares this balance of continuity and discontinuity, but it must be described differently. The new structure arises by the increase or heightening of some element or elements in the old structure. Such intensification may be very gradual, and it may be impossible to say at exactly what point the boundaries of the old structure are broken. Nevertheless, the relative strengthening of some element in the old can in the end lead to a regrouping of all the elements, bringing about a quite new range of possibilities for further development. The new structure is discontinuous with the old, although the process by which it came into being was continuous. This emergence of discontinuity within a continuous process will be called the crossing of a threshold.

Chapter Two turns from these general introductory reflections to a presentation of ontological and psychological ideas that underlie the descriptive treatments of the several structures of existence. Some aspects of the ontology are more fully and technically developed in Chapter II of *A Christian Natural Theology*. Although the categories of Whitehead's philosophy are constantly formative of the thought in this book as well, explicit use of his terminology is reduced to a minimum. This book should be generally intelligible apart from familiarity with Whitehead's philosophy, although a student of Whitehead will have a more precise understanding of the meaning at many points.

Even the psychological analysis is influenced by Whitehead, but it deals for the most part with problems he left untreated. I have not adopted any one psychology but have given my own order and definition to ideas that have become a part of lay psychology generally. The analysis has grown up in interaction with its application in distinguishing the several structures of existence. Hence, it in no way seeks completeness. It avoids those controversial issues, a treatment of which is not required by the argument, and it deals at length only with questions that become important in the application.

The basic application is made in Chapters Three through Ten. The question here is that of the choice of topics. Where in human development are the great thresholds crossed? The actual course of the development of new forms of existence is inconceivably complex, and every account, even the most detailed, is a high abstraction. In this case, where selected structural unities are sought behind the exceedingly diverse details, the abstraction is still more extreme. A brief explanation of the basis of selection and the organization of the material is needed.

First, and least controversial, is the judgment that with the rise of man a major threshold was crossed, not only biologically but also existentially or psychically. To understand that threshold, and thus our common heritage as men, we must form some notion of animal existence as well, so that both the continuity and the discontinuity can be understood.

Second, there was a major new beginning in human affairs in the fourth millennium before Christ. This is often called the rise of civilization. The way was paved for this development by the earlier rise of the Neolithic village. It is reasonable to suppose that parallel with these new developments in society there was also the emergence of a new structure of existence, a structure that distinguishes civilized man from his primitive ancestors.

Third, there is great value in Karl Jaspers' idea of an axial period.[6] Although a number of features of Jaspers' presentation are highly dubious, significantly similar developments in human existence did occur in the first millennium before Christ independently in China, India, Persia, Palestine, and Greece. This fact is of extraordinary importance for our total understanding of the history that has formed us. However, there was profound diversity among these cultures as well as similarity. It is more illuminating to speak of a plurality of structures of existence that proceeded to develop side by side — as well as to interact — rather than to speak of a single new structure of existence expressing itself in several forms. Furthermore, in Greece and Palestine there were further developments leading to the rise of still additional structures. The sharp distinction of Homeric and Socratic structures within the great diversity of modes of existence in Greece is a gross, but hopefully helpful, simplification. Much the same must be said of the parallel distinction of prophetic and Christian existence.

In addition to an account of what is common to the axial cultures, completeness would demand separate treatment of each of them as well as of the new structures to which their further development gave rise. However, since that is not practical, and since the major concern is to identify what is distinctive in Christianity, the discussion is chiefly focused on Greece and Israel. To broaden the range and indicate more sharply by contrast the peculiarities of both the Greek and the Palestinian developments, a brief treatment of India is included, with special reference to Buddhism. Among all the ancient traditions, Buddhism is Christianity's most serious competitor for modern man's attention and loyalty.

In the discussion of each culture, the majority of the space is de-

---

[6] Cf. *The Origin and Goal of History* (Yale University Press, 1953), pp. 1–21. See also the similar point made by Lewis Mumford, *The Transformations of Man* (Harper & Brothers, 1956), Ch. IV.

voted to a selective account of the beliefs and orientation of man in that culture. The selectivity is in terms of the purpose of highlighting that which expresses most clearly the peculiar structure of existence embodied in that culture. Some attempt is made to show how each culture arose by an accentuation of some element in its background and by a restructuring of existence around a new center. In concluding each chapter, I attempt to describe more directly the structure of existence as such.

The treatment of Christian existence, with which this series concludes, is somewhat longer than the others. Furthermore, it is supplemented by a separate chapter on love, which attempts to clarify the distinctiveness of Christian existence by comparative treatment of this essential element in it.

Although the selection and organization of the material throughout reflects the special interest in illuminating Christian existence and is undoubtedly influenced by its Christian perspective, the attempt in Chapters Three through Ten is to describe each structure of existence as objectively as possible. In Chapter Twelve attention is focused on comparison and relative evaluation as a means of justifying the Christian claim to finality.

Chapter Twelve introduces but does not discuss the important question of the emergence of new modes of existence in the centuries since the rise of Christian existence. The analysis of Western civilization in these terms would be fruitful, but it is not undertaken here. Concluding the study with Christian existence implies the judgment that despite the great variety of modes of existence that have appeared, and despite the great distance that separates us from primitive Christianity, a single structure is expressed in the whole of Christian history. However, we may have arrived at the end of the period for which such a designation is appropriate and for which such a judgment can be defended. An appraisal of the present situation with its many conflicting tendencies should be facilitated by the categories and the perspective developed in this book, but the task remains to be performed. In its absence, the implications of this study for our future must remain undeveloped.

Chapter Two

THE PSYCHE

THERE IS SUCH A THING as "conscious experience" or "awareness." I shall use the two expressions interchangeably. In one way or another all of us must begin with this, yet just for this reason it is impossible to define our terms. Both "conscious" and "experience" as primitive concepts cannot be explained by simpler terms and, as referring to the unique, cannot be classified as special cases under broader headings — as species under a known genus. The substitution of "awareness" does not alter this situation. However, this does not mean that nothing can be said to clarify and render more precise the particular way in which one chooses to use these terms, for here one finds real and significant variety. This variety is to be understood chiefly as a range of limits around a common center. When I direct focused attention on an object, a person, or an idea, seeking, thereby, an answer to a clearly formulated question, everyone is likely to agree that I am consciously experiencing that entity. Most of us would agree that conscious experience occurs also without such clearly focused interest, but just how far to extend the term is a matter of reasonable disagreement.

For example, one may feel a dull discomfort and yet ignore it; that is, one may turn attention elsewhere and proceed to think and act almost as if that discomfort were not there. Is the feeling at such times conscious? It is present to consciousness, we will suppose, in such a way that it is constantly making some claim to attention. If the other and temporarily dominant interest wanes, it will once again move into the center of attention. At such a time, one will recognize that the discomfort has been there all along. But in the meantime, while attention is directed away from this discomfort, should we call the continuing feeling conscious or not?

Or again, to take a very different question, what about dreams? Are they a part of conscious experience? Here the issue is not one of attention vs. inattention as a criterion of consciousness. There is no lack of attention to the subject matter of a vivid dream. The distinction here is the relation of the subject to his environment. " Conscious experience " is often limited to the type of awareness we have of the environment when we are awake and sober. But on such points ordinary usage is inconsistent, and the careful thinker must impose, more or less arbitrarily, his own consistent usage.

In this book " conscious experience " will be used as inclusively as possible. By this usage, " awareness " at any moment is broader than the focus of attention, and dreams are also a mode of " conscious experience." The first inclusion indicates that there are degrees of consciousness shading off into unconsciousness. One is more or less conscious of certain stimuli. The second indicates that there are different types of consciousness of equal vividness. Actually, this distinction between degrees and types of consciousness is itself oversimple. There is an endless variety of modes of awareness shading off into one another and into total nonawareness. Dream-consciousness is very different from ordinary waking-consciousness of the environment, but there are also experiences of many sorts that lie on the boundary between them. Nevertheless, classifications are necessary, and one useful distinction must now be made because of its importance for the analysis in the following chapters. This distinction is between conscious experience as significantly organized and conscious experience lacking such organization. The presupposition here is that although all consciousness depends on some organization of its contents, an organization that may be provided by the sense organs and related cerebral structures, this organization need not always be meaningful or significant. Examples and further comment may serve to make this assumption plausible and to explain the distinction.

I begin with an actual recent experience. I was riding in a train absorbed in a novel. My wife spoke to me, stating that we were near our destination. For a few seconds I continued reading, undisturbed by what she had said. Then, suddenly, her words " sank in " and

I hurriedly prepared to get off the train. At the moment that her words sank in, I realized that I had heard them several seconds earlier.

I regard the earlier hearing as a mode of awareness. That is, the sounds she uttered impinged upon my consciousness although my attention was directed elsewhere. Through the following moments, I remembered what I had heard, and finally their meaning registered in consciousness in such a way as to be recognized as requiring action. Now I am raising the question as to the status of these sounds in the seconds before their meaning sank in. There are two possible interpretations. One is that they carried their meaning with them from the beginning, but that this meaning failed at first to gain my attention. This is possible, and the experience would then *not* serve to illustrate the distinction between significantly organized experience and that which is not so organized. However, this is not the way it seemed to me at the time. It seemed, rather, that my original awareness was of sounds unassociated with meanings, and that when a few seconds later the memory of the sounds evoked their meaning, my attention was instantaneously redirected. If so, then we have an instance of awareness prior to significant organization. This type of awareness I will call " receptive " to indicate the absence of the psychic activity of meaningful ordering.

Clear examples of such receptive awareness in normal adult human experience are hard to find, for we cannot question our experience as to its contents without using signs. Nevertheless, such experience plays a large role. For example, we are somehow aware of everything in our field of vision, although our attention is much more narrowly focused. The focusing of attention is closely associated with significance, and much of what is not attended to in the visual field is also significantly ordered. Still, much of what is visually presented occurs simply as sensuously given and as otherwise quite meaningless. Novel significant organization is organization of such data, and if the data were not already there in experience, such a process could not occur. Also, it is possible to cultivate an awareness, even an attentive awareness, of these data that is free from such organization. Husserl's phenomenological method can be interpreted in these terms as can part of the technique of Zen Buddhism. All of this would be impossible if awareness were limited to what is significantly ordered.

That even attentive awareness does not presuppose such organization is indicated also by the response to a sudden loud noise. Such a noise forces itself into the center of attention and evokes certain emotional responses before any meaning is attached to it, before it is perceived even as a "loud noise." That this is so seems clear to introspection and is further substantiated by the behavior of babies.

The experience of babies is another indication of the fact and importance of awareness that is not significantly organized and of its separability from the question of attention. Infants attend to novel stimuli in their environment *before* they can deal significantly with them.

The evidence indicates that in the growth of conscious experience mere awareness is prior and primordial. In man the process of symbolization so transforms the whole that this prior and primordial experience recedes to the fringes of awareness and is only rarely and with difficulty brought to attention. However, both in the understanding of the relation of man to the subhuman and in the understanding of differences among structures of human existence, the distinction of significantly organized and receptive awareness plays an important role.

In the description of receptive awareness, the nature of significantly organized awareness has been indicated by contrast. In this awareness, elements of the environment, or the past, are perceived in terms of their relation to other entities, past, present, and future, or of their relevance to the experient subject. This relation or relevance is not a subsequent interpretation of data that are first passively received, but is, rather, the mode of initial conscious reception.

Conscious experience, then, includes both a diffuse receptive element and a significantly organized one. This latter can be subdivided according to the types of meaning it employs, and to this subject we will return in Chapter Three. First, however, it is important to broaden our understanding of experience by turning to its unconscious dimensions.

The vast majority of human experience is unconscious. This statement may seem extreme in view of the inclusiveness of the understanding of consciousness proposed above, but there is ample evidence

for its truth. Such evidence is provided by the depth psychologists
in their efforts to explain otherwise unintelligible aspects of conscious experience and behavior. But long before the time of Freud,
and with no reference to pathology, the fact was fully recognized.[7]
The primacy of unconscious activity can be seen even in reference
to the most conscious of mental activities, such as visual experience
of the environment and rational thought.

Physical and physiological science shows us something of the process
that eventuates in conscious vision. It begins with the emission or
reflection of light by objects in the external world. Light waves or
particles reach the human eye where they are not merely passively
but also actively received and translated into nervous impulses transmitted to the occipital lobe of the brain. These nerve impulses acti-
vate selected cells in this part of the brain.

Thus far the process is not one of the unconscious dimensions of
human experience but of external and bodily events. At this point,
however, the chain of bodily events is at an end, and we must consider the relation of the numerous cellular events in the brain to our
conscious visual experience. The chasm between these is a vast one.
On the one hand, we have a plurality of physical events located in-
side the brain. On the other hand, we have a unified conscious field
of vision located in the outside world. There must be extensive in-
termediate activity linking these two. Furthermore, much of this activity must have the kind of unity and creativity characteristic of
conscious experience. Yet in such experience we have no glimmer of
awareness of this activity. We can be aware in a general way of the
role of our eyes in mediating visual experience, but we have no
awareness of the work of the brain or of the process by which its
work is translated into our conscious experience. We are forced to
recognize that even the most passive of visual experiences are the
result of vast unconscious activity.

The situation with respect to thought is similar. When I am working out an argument such as this one, I am consciously thinking.
Indeed, when compared with my situation at most times, this is an
extreme case of conscious effort and control. Nevertheless, most of

---

[7] Cf., e.g., Lancelot Law Whyte, *The Unconscious Before Freud* (Double-
day & Company, Inc., 1962).

what takes place is unconscious.

For example, consider the use of words apart from which I would be quite unable to deal with the abstractions that are my stock-in-trade. At any given moment I am conscious of only a very few words, namely, those which at that moment I am using or about to use. Even if we suppose that the remainder of my vocabulary is somehow stored in my brain, I must confess that I have no conscious power to locate in my brain the words I desire and to bring them out. The words " come to me " more or less appropriately, more or less as they are needed. The way in which they come in one moment is influenced by vaguely conscious intentions and purposes of the preceding moment, but these intentions seem only to trigger processes that remain unconscious. If I am aware that there is a word that I want but that word does not come to me, I can consciously try various devices to facilitate its coming, but when and if it comes, it is supplied to consciousness by a process not itself conscious.

It is equally clear that the process of arriving at new ideas in terms of new conjunctions of words is chiefly unconscious. The idea, like the word, comes to consciousness and grows in consciousness by a process itself not consciously controlled. A person can consciously orient his attention in such a way as to facilitate this process or channel it. I am consciously aware of the results of these unconscious processes of thought as I am of the words that such processes also supply. But I am not conscious of the processes themselves.

The point at which consciousness plays its most autonomous role is in the judgment of the results of such processes. I can consciously consider the consistency and adequacy of the ideas proffered to me by my unconscious thought or by that of others. Logical and methodological reflection expresses the greatest independence that consciousness can achieve in thought. Yet even here the priority of the unconscious processes must be acknowledged. The conscious judgment that a certain argument or a certain type of argument is invalid is first the product of unconscious thought. Conscious reflection starts with such judgments and organizes them in relation to one another. It makes possible their extension to many cases where unconscious thought alone offers no conclusion. But it cannot ultimately explain its own activity.

I have intentionally chosen as examples those areas in which consciousness seems most autonomous to show that even there the conscious element is profoundly influenced by unconscious processes rather than being a self-contained entity or function. In other aspects of our experience, this is today less controversial. Few today would argue that the emotions of which we are conscious exhaust our emotional life or can be explained without reference to the ebb and flow of unconscious feeling.

Since no psychic activity is fully conscious, and all are dependent on unconscious functioning, the term " conscious activity " or " process " is misleading. Nevertheless, there is a distinction to be made, and this term is needed in order to make it. There are unconscious activities and processes that are but little affected by the forms and relations given to consciousness by the outside world. These are governed by aims at meaning and value that are often little oriented to the practical adaptation of the organism or the psyche to its environment. The results of these processes may or may not reach consciousness, in dreams or in waking life, but in either case they can be conveniently described as unconscious in their fundamental character. Alongside these are other psychic activities geared to man's conscious interaction with his environment and subject to a considerable measure of direction and control from the side of consciousness. These may conveniently be described as conscious despite the large unconscious component.

There are still those who reject the use of the term " experience " in any way more inclusive than conscious experience, and we must agree that the term derives its central connotation from such awareness. However, there is hardly an alternative to its extension. When we take conscious experience as our basis for understanding what experience is, we think of receiving and responding to stimuli from the body and the environment, of emotion, purpose, and thought, of the significant organization of data and the influencing of action. But all of this we must attribute also to the unconscious. All that is lacking is consciousness! We could, perhaps, create some word to represent a genus inclusive both of " experience," understood to mean consciousness, and of the unconscious. But to my knowledge no suitable word has yet been proposed. Furthermore, even then it would have to be recognized that the boundary between what would be called "experience" and the unconscious is vague and fluctuating, and that, for most purposes, they must be seen as constituting a unity. It is far more natural to use "experience" itself inclusively, distinguishing between its conscious and unconscious phases, when that distinction is important for the question at issue.

I have tried to make clear that I do *not* regard the unconscious as identical with the brain or any other entity subject to direct investigation by the physiologist. The prejudice in favor of a physiological explanation of experience, and especially of unconscious experience, has long been very great. But this prejudice is to be understood as the result of a metaphysical faith rather than any actual evidence. If one assumes that only what can be seen and felt is "real," and that everything else, including the subjective seeing and feeling, must be a function of this reality, then psychology *must* be reducible to physiology. The fact that the most fruitful research has occurred only when this dogma has been denied (or bracketed, as by Freud) is not yet viewed as any grounds for lesser faith, nor are the extraordinary paradoxes that follow from this dogma for thought's understanding of itself. On the other hand, every correlation between physiological functioning and subjective experience (and I assume that far more such correlation will be discovered in the future) is hailed as proof that eventually the reduction of psychology to physiology and biology will be achieved.

The power of this dogma over intelligent minds rests not on its own plausibility, usefulness, or attractiveness but on the unacceptability of what are supposed to be the only alternatives. The Cartesian dualism of mental and physical substances is indeed unacceptable, as is the idealism that reduces the physical to the function of the mental. Also, the popular idea of a mysterious, nonphysical, immortal soul temporarily attached to the body is unacceptable. In other scientific disciplines, the road of progress has been the road of sensuous observation with its implicit assumption that the primary and determinative reality is what is sensuously given. Hence, the prejudice is understandable.

Nevertheless, the prejudice is *not* acceptable. It is simply not the case that everything real is visible and tangible. The physicist today understands the whole world as made up of entities that can affect his senses only in very indirect ways. Furthermore, these entities resist interpretation as being like visible and tangible entities, only smaller. They function in ways quite different from such entities. Visible and tangible entities must finally be understood as functions of these quite different entities — not vice versa. If we are to avoid dualism — and that is also my desire [8] — we must get our monistic model elsewhere than from the objects of sensuous experience. In such a situation, the bias in favor of understanding unconscious experience as a function of the brain loses whatever metaphysical justification it may once have had.

However, neither the analogy of the physicist's particles nor the direct evidence justifies the idea of a mental substance. In the first place, by no means all the functioning of the unconscious is " mental " in any ordinary sense. In the second place, the notion of substance introduces the idea of stable endurance through time — if not of a wholly unempirical and unthinkable something — which is not called for by the evidence. There are continuities within the unconscious, but they are the kinds of continuities to be found within a process. What is to be affirmed, in affirming the unconscious, is a succession of experiences in which continuity is established by reenactment rather than by static identity.

In the foregoing I have written too often as if consciousness and the unconscious constituted separate entities rather than aspects of a single entity or process. It is, at times, convenient to use these nouns to refer collectively to all those elements of experience describable respectively by the adjectives "conscious" and "unconscious," and I will resort to this usage from time to time. I hope, however, it is clear that the real entity or process of which I am speaking is a unity of which much is always unconscious and of which a small part is sometimes conscious. It is this exceedingly complex process and the various structures which it embodies that constitute the subject matter of this book.

This process can be referred to in various ways. The two that will

---

[8] Here, as elsewhere, I follow Whitehead. The reader interested in seeing how this works out in a doctrine of man can consult the first two chapters of my *A Christian Natural Theology*.

be found most commonly in this book are, on the one hand, psyche or soul and, on the other, existence. In general, when this process is being viewed objectively as one of the many processes that constitute the world as a whole or the psychophysical organism which is man, psyche or soul is more appropriate. When, instead, attention is directed to this same process as it exists for itself, in its immediacy and subjectivity, existence is employed. The decision to take " structure of existence " rather than " structure of the psyche " as the key concept for the book as a whole reflects the desire to direct *primary* attention to the subjectivity of the process. But it is the mutual illumination of the subjective and the objective, the inner and the outer, rather than their separation that distinguishes the analysis here offered. Hence, no sharp distinction is to be expected with respect to terminology.

I use also at times the term " occasion of experience." This is a Whiteheadian term, and my use of it expresses my acceptance of and dependence on Whitehead's analysis of process. He holds that the process which is a man's experience through time is composed of atomic units. The process as a whole is the succession of these atomic units which are the individual occasions of human experience. An occasion of human experience is human existence at a moment.

In Whitehead's view (and mine), occasions of experience are not limited to the human ones. Even in the psychophysical organism there are many other processes consisting of such occasions besides the one that constitutes the psyche or human existence. When the stress is on the role of the occasions constituting the psyche in relation to the other occasions transpiring in the organism, then the adjective " dominant " is sometimes placed before " occasion of experience." Also in the case of animals, it is often best to speak of dominant occasions of experience to refer to that entity which in man is organized as soul.

The concept of occasion of experience enables us to see what is common to the human soul and all other entities whatsoever. The concept of dominant occasion of experience enables us to see in what further respects the human soul resembles its counterpart in other animals. For a total evolutionary view, the former would be of utmost importance. For this book, in which the earlier stages of the process are neglected, the latter is of special importance, as will appear in the next chapter.

Ontologically speaking, the dominant occasion of experience is not different from the other occasions of experience with which it jointly constitutes the psychophysical animal organism. It plays, however, a unique role in the organism, and to play this role it must have vastly greater complexity. It occurs only where a developed central nervous system is to be found, and it receives its primary data from this nervous system. Its basic function is to relate stimuli received in this way to the effective organs in such a way that the organism can respond appropriately to changes in its environment.

Of all the occasions in the animal organism, only the dominant occasion enjoys consciousness. However, much of its functioning does not require consciousness and not all dominant occasions of experience participate in consciousness at all. Thus even for the dominant occasion of experience, unconsciousness is the basic mode of its being.

The dominant occasion of experience is related not only to the other occasions jointly constituting the physical organism, such as the entities making up the brain, but also to past dominant occasions of experience in the same organism. The relative importance of the relation to the body and the relation to the past dominant occasions varies. At one extreme, we can posit the occurrence of an actual occasion of experience that receives stimuli and triggers motor responses without any significant influence of prior dominant occasions. At the other extreme, we can imagine an occasion in which new stimuli from the body are negligible and the memory of past occasions decisive. Most dominant occasions fall somewhere on the continuum between these two extremes. The place on this continuum is an important element in determining the structures of existence to be described in the following chapters.

Chapter Three

PRIMITIVE EXISTENCE

THE PURPOSE OF THIS CHAPTER is to describe what distinguishes the structure of human existence in general from the structure of subhuman animal existence in general. Since the human developed out of the subhuman, and since this process of development was a continuous one, it is essential to understand what man has in common with other animals, as well as to describe the threshold that marked his appearance as something genuinely and decisively new. The attempt in this account is not to offer a description of the complex diversity of animal and human life, but only to describe types of structures that are to be found within each.

Animals give evidence of both instinct and intelligence. By instinct is meant ordered and predictable behavior to which learning is irrelevant; and by intelligence, the capacity to learn. Human intelligence has other ingredients, some of which are also shared by some animals, but, in general, intelligence among animals can be measured by the speed of learning and the complexity of what is learned.

Instinct and intelligence are complexly interrelated in most animals, and they are not wholly to be contrasted. What is now instinctive may have once been learned by ancestors. Instinctive tendencies may be inhibited by new experience and a different behavior can be learned. Nevertheless, a clear difference exists, and it is possible to formulate the distinctive role and structure of the dominant occasions of experience in the two cases in the categories worked out in the preceding chapter.

For the occurrence of purely instinctive behavior, the dominant occasion of experience functions only as a switchboard. It receives a stimulus either from the environment or from some part of the body. It communicates this stimulus to some center in the brain which then governs the response. In carrying out the response, additional external stimuli may be relevant, and in this sense the occasion of experience may continue to play a role. But what that role is and how it is played are determined by the physical structures in the central nervous system.

The closest approximations to *purely* instinctive behavior are to be found among insects. There is no reason to deny consciousness to insects. Aspects of the external world appear to register on them, as in the receptive consciousness of man. What is lacking is any significant organization of experience. The relevant sensory stimulus is not interpreted as signifying something. It is simply registered and transmitted, thereby triggering an automatic response predetermined by the structure of the central nervous system. What occurs in each moment is determined by the stimuli of that moment rather than by the cumulative impact of preceding experiences.

If learning takes place, either the central nervous system must be physically changed by new stimuli or new experiences must be influenced by earlier ones. Both may occur. However, it is doubtful that learning could ever be explained purely on the basis of the former, whereas the second by itself can suffice. Hence, we shall focus upon this one.

Before learning can occur, stimuli must function as signals.[9] A signal is a stimulus that is taken as indicating the presence or occurrence of something else, something of more importance than itself. For example, a particular odor or sound, of no importance in itself, is taken by an animal as indicating the presence of another animal. The presence of this other animal may be of great im-

---

[9] I take my distinction of signals and symbols from Susanne Langer, *Philosophy in a New Key,* third edition (Harvard University Press, 1957), especially Chapter III. I refer the reader to that book for a much fuller account. I use " signals " instead of " signs " in consideration of Miss Langer's statement in the " Preface to the Edition of 1951," where she indicates that Charles Morris' terminology has advantages over her own. " Signs " should then be inclusive of both signals and symbols, and I am using " signify " and " significant " in this inclusive sense.

portance as a source of food or a threat to life.

There may sometimes be an instinctive base to the response to such signals. That would mean that the brain, prior to experience, is so structured as to cause the appropriate response as soon as the stimulus is received and independently of its interpretation. However, at least in the higher animals, such responses can be overcome by association of other entities with the signal. Innumerable new stimuli can become signals through learned association. Hence, clearly the stimulus is not simply related to a physical center, but is also interpreted as a signal. We have to do with a much more complex operation of the dominant occasion of experience, an operation of interpretation and organization rather than simply of passive reception and transmission.

Moreover, the interpretation and significant organization of experience is in terms of memory of past experiences. Memory does not mean here conscious recall, although that need not always be totally excluded. It does mean that an important factor influencing the interpretation of new stimuli in the present is past experience. It means that what happens in the present experience will influence the interpretation of future stimuli. The beginning of that continuity of experience from birth to death which allows us to speak of *a* psyche or soul is there. The degree of such continuity, the extent of its importance in the formation of each new moment of experience, may differ greatly. When we compare the higher primates with the insects, this continuity is very great indeed. Yet even among them the content of each momentary experience seems generally to be more determined by the present deliverances of the sense organs than by its bond to predecessor and successor experiences. An ape, which is capable of using a stick to reach a banana when it sees the stick and bananas together, cannot do so when it sees them successively.[10]

To an overwhelming extent, the animal psyche exhausts itself in its service to the organism. In the case of the higher animals, this service requires a considerable activity on its part, both conscious and unconscious. This activity can be effectively performed only as past experience can cumulatively provide help in the interpretation

[10] *Ibid.*, pp. 126 and 135. (On page 126, reference is made to Köhler, *The Mentality of Apes*, p. 37.)

of present experience. All of this has a thoroughly functional role, fully intelligible in terms of survival value.

The question now arises as to whether this highly organized and active psyche performs any of its actions for its own enjoyment or enhancement and independent of its contribution to the welfare of the organism as a whole. For the great majority of animals the answer is probably that it does not. The pleasure of the psyche is a function of the well-being of the physical organism, and it seeks no other pleasure. However, there is evidence that among the higher primates there is the emergence of a small amount of nonfunctional psychic activity. Here again I appeal to Susanne Langer's evidence, which consists largely in noting cases of irrational fear on the part of chimpanzees, fear that cannot be explained either by instinct or by learning. She writes, in addition, of a case in which an ape could be consoled for the absence of its master by presenting it with a garment.[11]

All of this points to the minimal presence in the higher primates of a capacity for what I call the autonomous development of the psyche. Autonomous development involves two elements. First, the aim at intensity or richness of experience on the part of individual moments of the soul's life leads the soul to actualize itself in ways that are immediately rewarding to it, independently of their consequences for the organism as a whole. Second, successive occasions build upon the achievements of their predecessors, in this respect, in such a way as significantly to modify the behavior of the organism as a whole. The behavior of the apes indicates that at least some surplus psychic energy is available for autonomous activity, although its use and expression are so random that we cannot affirm that an autonomous development actually takes place.

The distinction of man from all other animals is that in him autonomous development assumes great importance. As with all the thresholds crossed in the evolutionary process leading to man and in the further development of man, we do not have the sudden emergence of an element previously totally lacking. We may assume that the simian ancestors of man were in this respect far more

11 Langer, *op. cit.,* pp. 110–115.

developed than any present-day ape. If we had before us all the crea-
tures in the evolutionary development, we would not be able to say
at exactly what point we are confronted by the first man. The transition would be too gradual. Nevertheless, we can say that at that point
at which the surplus psychic energy became sufficient in quantity to
enable the psychic life to become its own end rather than primarily
a means to the survival and health of the body, the threshold was
crossed dividing man from the animal. Man is that being in which
the psyche aims at its own well-being. Since that well-being largely
depends on the survival, health, and comfort of the body, the psyche
continues in man to serve these. But the human psyche also seeks
its satisfaction in ways that have nothing to do with the functional
needs of the body and even in ways that are detrimental to the body.

The great primary increase in man's psychic activity was unconscious. The primordial role of consciousness was to relate the organism to its environment through the reception of stimuli and their
interpretation as signals. Even in this functioning, unconscious processes play a large role, and hence we must attribute unconscious
experience also to animals. These functions continued in man, and
man's increased ability to learn and his improved manual dexterity
enabled him to make better practical responses to these stimuli.
Nevertheless, it was not these practical advantages that constituted
man's true distinctiveness, but rather the greatly increased unconscious psychic activity organizing the whole of experience for its own
sake.

The data with which the unconscious operated in its quest for
significant organization of the psychic life included the content of
the receptive consciousness as well as signals and their conscious
interpretation. But they included also the whole welter of conscious
and unconscious emotions and feelings from the past as well as the
cumulative results of previous psychic activity. In addition, they included material received directly from the psychic life of others. These
materials were combined with each other in all manner of ways, but
it is important to see that the guiding principle of such organization
was not practical usefulness in the adaptation to the environment, but
intrinsic satisfaction. The modes in which organization was achieved

did not altogether exclude those we would call rational, but these were far from primary.

This whole process of psychic activity is one of symbolization. Symbols, unlike signals, have their meaning independently of the presence or absence of what is symbolized. They connote ideas, concepts, and one another rather than simply denoting some other entity. The process of symbolization is one of giving new material its place in relation to the old. For primitive symbolization, whether the source of the material was in the external world or in private experience was irrelevant.

With the growth of symbolization, practically the whole of conscious experience was symbolically organized. This meant that it was given meanings and placed in relation with other elements of experience according to principles of association and interpretation spontaneously generated in the unconscious life independently of pragmatic value. Since these symbol systems in their most important expressions were social products, their communication and use placed some check upon the freedom of unconscious fantasy, and this is clear if we compare them with dreams. Nevertheless, they are to be understood primarily as expressions of the unconscious mind, designed to satisfy unconscious needs, rather than as conscious responses to conscious questions.

Alongside this rich symbolic growth lay the continuing operation of intelligence in the interpretation of signals and the devising of new responses. In this area practical success and failure were decisive. Men learned from trial and error.

In our attempt to understand primitive man, we must think of these two psychic activities together. Each involved both consciousness and unconsciousness, but in different ways. Symbolization occurred in the unconscious, taking the data supplied largely by consciousness and ordering them in symbols only partly influenced by the forms present in the data. This in turn produced a symbolically ordered consciousness. The intelligent interpretation and response to signals, on the other hand, originated in the receptive consciousness. The association on which it was based was determined by the association given to that consciousness by the external world. Unconscious processes played a role as they do in relation to all consciousness, but in this case checked and controlled by results in and for consciousness.

Of these two modes of psychic activity, the intelligent interpretation and response to signals was prior, since it was in continuity with animal existence. For man, however, symbolization was primary. It encompassed everything, including the practical dealing with the environment, overlaying it with new meaning and relating it thereby with the rest of experience.

The dominance of the symbolization based on unconscious processes was as often inhibiting of intelligent action as it was productive of it. Because of their symbol systems, men have, at times, failed to respond to novel challenges and have preferred, instead, simply to be destroyed. Thus the value of the symbol has little to do initially with any improved ability to deal practically with the environment. Yet it is easily confused in the primitive mentality with such capacity. Symbolization and magic go hand in hand and remain associated quite independently of the empirical evidence supporting the claimed power. On the contrary, whereas the effectiveness of signals is directly correlated with the actual experience of the environment, the power and intrinsic value of symbols is so great that they can withstand what appears to us as counterevidence for hundreds and even thousands of years without weakening. This is possible partly because the symbols determine the interpretation of the evidence insofar as what we would call evidence is relevant at all. But it is true also because the symbol does give to man immense psychic power — the power to bring together past and present in conscious memory and to relate and order what is otherwise simply given.

This symbolic ordering of experience, although primarily unconscious, gave rise to a new and incomparably richer mode of consciousness. This we will call the "reflective consciousness." Animal consciousness contained receptive and significant elements, but these latter were almost entirely limited to signals. By the use of symbols, consciousness could order and fill with meaning far larger portions of what it received. It could relate this to a context that included both past and future. It could preserve its achievements through symbolized memory and thus gain a new possibility of cumulative growth.

The reflective consciousness need not be rational.[12] Indeed for primitive man, rationality played a minor role. The reflective consciousness was chiefly a function of unconscious processes in relation to which it had little autonomy.

Although the term "myth" applies strictly to only some portions of this primitive symbolic activity, I shall speak of the whole as mythical and characterize primitive man's existence as mythical existence. By mythical existence I mean, then, an existence that satisfies two conditions. First, reflective consciousness supersedes receptive awareness and the organization of experience in terms of signals. Second, the symbolization involved is governed by modes of creation and association characteristic of the unconscious and not subject to testing against receptive awareness.

Mythical thinking is not to be thought of primarily as an attempt to explain the external world, for such a concept presupposes a consciousness of the duality of subject and object, internal and external, which is not characteristic of the mythical mentality. Nevertheless, if we view it in terms of *our* distinction of internal and external, we can highlight certain features in a useful way. From this point of view, the mythical mind engaged in a great deal of projection. This should not be difficult for us to understand, since this is also a large part of our own way of understanding significant elements in the environment. Its presence in our own experience is illustrated by the use of projective techniques by psychologists as a means of learning about our unconscious. They confront us with inkblots or with somewhat indeterminate pictures and ask us to tell what we see. It would, of course, be possible to respond to such a demand by very exact description of what is objectively there to be seen, that is, what is given in receptive awareness, but this is not what the psychologist means, and the success of the test indicates that, in fact, we "see" a great deal in our environment independently of its determinate presence there. The strange shapes of the inkblots or the indeterminate figures in the drawings present themselves to us in terms of definite meanings, which we unconsciously project on them. It is clear that in our relations with other people and groups, they are

---

[12] Discussion of the meaning of "rational" is postponed to the next chapter.

often the occasion but not the cause of a great deal of what we perceive in them. Much of what we see in one another is unconsciously
projected by each upon the other.

Today through careful and prolonged reflection, often requiring
the aid of a trained counselor, we may gain considerable ability to
distinguish between that which comes from our unconscious symbolization and the external reality we confront, although even the
most rational of us should be very hesitant about claiming much
success. Ancient man could not conceptualize such distinctions. His
total experience was, from our point of view, a selective synthesis
of the outer and the inner worlds, but for him the experience was
simply given with its meanings indissolubly a part of the whole.
There was little distinction of inner and outer, subject and object; little distinction between those elements of the experience contributed by the more remote past and those contributed by present
occurrences. There was a single meaningful whole. The meaning of
the whole was primarily determined by symbols arising out of the
unconscious aspects of experience. There was no second-level critical
reflection about these meanings. Hence, they were absolute.

We can find other aspects of our present experience that help us
to understand the mythical mentality of our ancestors.

Which of us in talking to children has not at times said: "People
don't do that," or, "Boys aren't supposed to do that." When we say
this in a certain tone of voice and with sufficient finality, it seems
to settle the question. Many of us are very sure that certain things
are not to be done, even though when pressed we are hard put to
find effective explanations. Indeed, we may regard the demand for
an explanation as a kind of absurdity or even sacrilege. Some things,
we think, are simply beyond such questioning, and the person who
does not see things that way is lacking in essential humanity.

This means, of course, that for us, too, some things are still sacred.
Our reaction toward the prospect of eating human flesh or having
sexual intercourse with our parents transcends, in its violence, any
rational justification we may subsequently give for our views. Yet
we are the most secularized generation ever to walk upon the earth!
One wonders if the time is coming when men will be unable to
achieve any empathy at all toward the sense of the sacred —— the

" ought " that is prior to and independent of any justification. In any case, since most of us can recognize such feelings in ourselves, we do have a starting point for empathizing with a very different kind of human existence in which every feature of life was determined in great detail by the sense of the sacred. A man must do in each situation that which men have always done, that which was originally done, or simply that which *is* done. Even today, we often ask, What is one to do in a given situation? and we mean, What do people do? For primitive man there could hardly be another question.

Alongside projection and the sense of the sacred, we can find other aspects of our experience that we share with the mythical mentality. The poet and artist, as well as the psychologist, sometimes make use of an association of symbols quite different from that of controlled scientific and philosophical thought. We continue to take occasional delight in the fantasy of fairy tales and cartoons. Our dreams bring us in contact with still stranger workings of the unconscious, and our daydreams are often patently wishfulfilling.

More important than all this, in spite of our urbanization, we still feel in our depths something of the rhythm of the seasons, their endlessly varied but repetitive recurrence, the wonder of new beginning each spring. We still feel some need to celebrate the great events of birth and death and marriage. When things go wrong, we still seek explanations in a more than factual sphere. Our need for scapegoats has not declined. For us as for our tribal ancestors, the world is divided into " our kind " and the others, and we invent strange stories to tell ourselves in order to justify our hatred or fear of the others. In these and many other ways, we can feel our cohumanity with our ancient ancestors. Nevertheless, the basic structure of our existence differs from theirs, and we will trace the emergence of this difference in the following chapters.

Before concluding this chapter, however, something should be said explicitly about oral language. Symbolization is much broader than language, but language is by far its most important form. The further developments in the structures of existence, which are described in subsequent chapters, are wholly dependent on language.

There are many theories about the rise of language, but in relation to the analysis offered in this chapter, the question can be simply posed. Did language arise in the attempt to communicate about signals and to invent additional signals, gradually developing beyond signals into genuine symbols? Or did language arise as a part of the nonpragmatic activity of the psyche? If a choice must be made between these alternatives, the latter is certainly preferable. Since for the primitive mentality the world of symbolization was far more inclusive than that of practical adjustment to the environment, it would be surprising if so pervasive a factor as language were not a part and product of it. Furthermore, the actual use and form of language renders it very difficult to understand as primarily practical in origin. Nevertheless, there is no real necessity for choosing. Is it not likely that man's extraordinary capacity for making sounds and his spontaneous pleasure in doing so influenced both sides of his psychic life?

The structure of primitive existence may now be summarily described as follows. It continued the receptive awareness and the consciousness in terms of signals structurally unchanged. It added an immense richness to the unconscious, which, by the continuity of its life, constituted the successive occasions of human experience as a unified soul. This unconscious life was characterized by a vast autonomous development, which in its turn brought into being the reflective consciousness. This was organized by means of the symbols developed in the unconscious. Thus the older and more primitive aspects of consciousness continued relatively independent of the unconscious, while the new and dominant segment of consciousness was itself primarily a function of the unconscious.

Chapter Four

CIVILIZED EXISTENCE

TERMS SUCH AS " primitive " and " archaic " lack clear demarcations. Furthermore, in the continuous process of development, any such demarcations are arbitrary. However, in the Neolithic period we find the presence of a culture to which the word " primitive " does not readily apply. There were settled communities that had domesticated both plants and animals and possessed highly developed skills in various arts and crafts. This type of community life we will call " archaic," and thereby differentiate it from earlier modes of existence before stable communities, domestication of plants and animals, and skilled craftsmanship had arisen.

The term " civilization " we will reserve for a still further stage of cultural development —that in which cities were built. The building of cities required additional technical advances, but primarily it required new forms of social organization. Whereas primitive and archaic cultures required little specialization of functions and little work beyond that required to provide food, clothing, and shelter, civilization required a high degree of specialization and a great amount of disciplined labor directed to providing wealth for the community as a whole and for a small class within it.

The transitions from primitive to archaic culture and from archaic culture to civilization were, of course, gradual. But in general, we may guess that archaic culture emerged for the first time in the eighth millennium before Christ and civilization in the fourth. In both cases we can trace the spread of culture from certain early centers, but we can also see that it emerged independently in widely separated places and at different times.

I have grouped these two stages of human development together because, despite the great sociological differences between them, I see them as expressing a single continuous process in the development of human existence. This process is that of the rationalization of the reflective consciousness. If we related this process to the sociological phenomena, we would probably find that, whereas in archaic culture this process involved the whole community more or less equally, in civilized societies it was greatly accelerated in certain social classes and retarded in the mass of workers on which such societies rested. However, I shall not attempt to pursue this kind of analysis. Instead, I intend only to treat the one question as to what is involved in the emergence of the rational consciousness. For this purpose I shall focus attention on civilized existence, simply acknowledging that the process described was already far advanced before the advent of civilization.

In Chapter Two, we considered the nature of consciousness in order to gain the basis for an understanding of the major stages of human development. In addition to the vast complexity of unconscious experience, I suggested, we can analyze conscious experience into significantly organized and receptive levels. In Chapter Three, we distinguished further between significant organization by signals and by symbols. Whereas we can posit the presence of receptive consciousness wherever a developed central nervous system is to be found in the animal world, and of organization by signals wherever learning is possible, symbolic organization of consciousness or reflective consciousness depends on the power of symbolization, which is the distinguishing characteristic of man.

Civilization depends on and makes possible a high degree of rationalization of the reflective consciousness. By rationality I do not mean the self-consciousness about the principles of thought that is expressed in explicit logic or reflection about methodology. I mean, instead, the kind of thinking that logic, in its most elementary forms, attempts to bring to self-consciousness. The process of such thinking is initially and primarily unconscious, yet it differs profoundly from mythical thinking. It conforms, for example, albeit unconsciously, to the principle of noncontradiction, whereas contradictions disturb the mythical mentality but little.

Rationality is not to be identified with intelligence, although it cannot occur apart from a high level of intelligence. Intelligence is the capacity to learn from experience and to develop more appropriate and functional responses. As such it emerged very early in the course of animal life. Some animals are more intelligent than others, and man is probably the most intelligent of all. This capacity to learn from experience in man, as in other animals, is primarily bound up with the interpretation of signals and with the ability to bring past experience to bear on present interpretation.

In primitive existence, intelligent adaptation to the environment and unconscious symbolization, as a means of intensifying and ordering the psychic life, existed side by side. Consciousness contained both the awareness of stimuli and the interpretation of signals as well as the inclusive overlay of a new, reflective level. On the one side, there was intelligence; on the other, the use of symbols. Neither in itself constituted rationality.

Nevertheless, the conjoint presence of intelligence and symbolization provided for the possibility of the rational consciousness. Rationality emerged whenever the process of symbolization was controlled by intelligence or whenever intelligence made use of symbols instead of mere signals in its interpretation of the environment. Since the two levels of the primitive mind were not rigidly separated from one another, we should expect some rationalization of the reflective consciousness from a very early point. But before the rise of archaic culture, the role of rationality was very limited. The reflective consciousness, which is the most striking factor differentiating man from other animals, was the by-product of unconscious processes and initially fully subordinate to them. As long as this subordination existed, the reflective consciousness could not interpenetrate effectively with the other dimensions of conscious significance. The effective rationalization of the reflective consciousness required the attainment by the reflective consciousness of a high degree of autonomy.

The process by which the reflective consciousness achieved such autonomy is analogous to that in which the psyche as a whole entered into autonomous development. It is, indeed, a further step in the same continuous process of psychic growth — the crossing of another threshold. In the earlier process, the dominant occasion of animal experience ceased to function purely for the sake of the animal body and began to develop activities for its own enrichment independent of their functional value for the organism. These activities conformed to entirely new patterns, patterns of which even today we have only a little understanding. This new activity brought into being a new mode of consciousness, the reflective consciousness, which integrated the externally given world of the receptive consciousness with the world of unconscious symbolization. But once the reflective consciousness existed, it embodied an immense new value in itself, so that a psychic life aimed at its own heightened richness tended to aim at the enhancement and strengthening of this new mode of consciousness. Insofar as this heightening of the reflective consciousness occurred, it necessarily increased the role of the forms that are given in the receptive consciousness and, hence, their influence on the reflective consciousness and the symbolization by which it lives. To whatever degree the symbols and their association were correlated with what was given in the receptive consciousness, symbolization could be checked and developed through a process of learning from experience. That meant that it could become intelligent; it could be employed for the interpretation of signals and greatly increase the power and range of such interpretation. In short, that marriage of intelligence with symbolization could occur which constitutes rationality.

The reflective consciousness is necessarily symbolic, primordially mythical, but incipiently rational. It is necessarily symbolic, because reflection is possible only in symbols. It is primordially mythical, because the process of symbolization was originally unconscious and determined by the laws of psychic satisfaction as such. It is incipiently rational, because its attention is directed to data supplied by the receptive consciousness, and insofar as the reflective consciousness becomes free from the dominance of the unconscious, these data must play a larger and more direct role in their own interpretation.

Prior to the rise of the great civilizations of antiquity, from the fourth millennium before Christ on, rationality played a minor role in human life. That did not mean that there were not individuals with considerable rational ability. At least in the later millennia of this long development we may assume that there were many men capable of relatively sustained rational reflection. Nevertheless, the effects of this rational activity on existence as a whole were minor. The signs that such reasoning did begin to restructure man's relations with the environment and with his fellowman are precisely those remains which represent to us the emergence of civilization. Furthermore, the conditions of civilization demanded and encouraged an immense increase in the role of rationality. Hence, it is my thesis that correlative with the rise of civilization in Egypt, Mesopotamia, India, China, and, later, in Mexico and Peru, a new psychic threshold was crossed. Men could observe, calculate, plan, and organize on an entirely new scale, opening up a new range of possibilities, both externally and inwardly. Mathematics, astronomy, architecture, law, education, medicine, and government emerged as quite new outward achievements of a reflective consciousness freed to think in terms of meanings given by the structures in the observable world. Important and increasing areas of the existence of many individuals were dominated by this rationalized aspect of the reflective consciousness.

Nevertheless, the dominant mentality in these great ancient civilizations remained mythical. Just as in primitive man intelligent interpretation of signals continued alongside the more comprehensive reflective consciousness, so now the rational consciousness came into being alongside the mythical consciousness, but without overthrowing its inclusive dominance. In the astronomy of civilized man, careful observation, intelligent generalization, and accurate prediction played a large and impressive role. But the motivation of the astronomy, its interpretation, and its integration into the whole of reflective consciousness were predominantly mythical. Similarly, the complex organization of government could not have arisen or been adapted to new needs apart from the extensive rationalization of consciousness. Yet the ultimate understanding of government and of the persons of the rulers was mythical.

What, then, shall we say of the structure of existence in ancient civilized man? It continued to be mythical in the sense that the reflective consciousness continued to be dominantly determined in its comprehensive functioning by the activity of unconscious symbolization. But it gained also extensive autonomy, and that meant that in large segments of its activity it was rational. With the emergence of rationality as an important factor in human existence, a whole new range of possibilities arose.

Chapter Five

AXIAL EXISTENCE

A NUMBER OF OBSERVERS have noted that in the middle part of the millennium before Christ a new type of thinking arose, reflecting a new type of existence. What is most striking is that this occurred independently in five parts of the Eurasian continent at more or less the same time. During the sixth century before Christ, lived Confucius and Lao-tzu in China, Gautama Buddha in India, and Zoroaster in Persia. In the same century, Thales and Pythagoras were founding Greek philosophy, and the prophetic movement in Israel reached a climax in Second Isaiah.

Karl Jaspers has proposed that we extend the period of our attention to the six centuries from 800 B.C. to 200 B.C. and call this the "axial period." [13] The basic modes of thought and existence that even today compete for our attention and loyalty, he argues, arose in that period.

Jaspers' view requires correction in several directions. He presents this change in man's existence as if it were wholly unparalleled, whereas it was, in fact, the crossing of a new threshold in a succession of threshold crossings. He focuses attention on what was common in the axial existence of the several cultures in such a way as to neglect the diversity, whereas that diversity is just as important to our understanding of our present situation as is what was common. He stresses the unity of the change also in such a way as to conceal

[13] *The Origin and Goal of History,* p. 1. Jaspers' choice of this term for this period is intended as criticism of the Christian view that the center of universal history is Jesus Christ. In what follows it will become clear that the adoption of the term here does not entail agreement with Jaspers' view of the historical role of Jesus.

the successive stages within some of the axial revolutions. He closes the period before the rise of Christianity, wheras this too constituted a further threshold in the history of man's existence. He presents axial man in such sharp contrast with preaxial man that the continuity of the historical process and the numerous foreshadowings of axial man in the preceding centuries are obscured.

Despite all this, Jaspers is correct in seeing the developments of the first millennium before Christ as of utmost importance for human existence. New structures of existence did come into being during that period. Furthermore, despite their diversity, at a certain level of abstraction one can also note their common features. Jaspers' term "axial" is useful for referring to this common element of structure, and it is this common structure that I propose to describe in this chapter. Later chapters will describe selected examples in their distinctness from one another.

What distinguished axial man was the new role of rationality in the structure of his existence. This newness, with its consequences, was so great that we can appreciate the sense of marvel which Jaspers communicates to his reader in his account of it. Nevertheless, we can understand its continuity and discontinuity with the ancient civilizations that preceded it as fully analogous with the continuity and discontinuity of these civilizations with primitive man. The reflective consciousness, through thousands of years of civilization, became increasingly rational in widening areas. There were many individuals who came to be increasingly at home in this world of rational consciousness and increasingly estranged from the mythical world that still controlled their situation. Finally, men appeared who, from the perspective of this strengthened rationality, could effectively destroy the power of the mythical world not only for themselves but for many others as well. This drastic break with the mythical age constituted the axial period. The new kind of existence that it expressed and created constituted axial existence. The cultures and religions to which this new existence gave rise are the axial cultures and religions, which still dominate the world. The axial men who embody this existence and participate in these cultures are ourselves.

To explain more precisely what occurred in the crossing of this threshold, a new category is required. Thus far we have distinguished the unconscious, receptive consciousness, and significantly organized consciousness. In man we have seen that symbolization superseded organization by signals as the predominant mode of significantly organized consciousness, and that this constituted reflective consciousness. The categories of reflective consciousness were influenced by the unconscious and by the receptive consciousness. This structure is common for all men. The change that occurred with the rise of civilization was that the influence of the receptive consciousness on the symbols of the reflective consciousness grew stronger, but without destroying the overall dominance of the unconscious.

The new category now required is that of the " seat of existence." The psychic life as a whole continued to be primarily unconscious and had its own centers of organization that remained unknown to consciousness. But reflective consciousness gained a unity of its own. This unity was achieved around some center or some determining perspective, and it is this center that is the seat of existence. This center can be either in consciousness or in the unconscious. When it is in the unconscious, then the rational activities of reflective consciousness are incorporated into the whole life of the psyche only in terms of mythical meanings. When it is in reflective consciousness, then the products of the unconscious appear as strange and alien powers to be feared and obeyed or examined and analyzed.

The locus of the seat of existence in reflective consciousness does not guarantee its control over all that takes place within that consciousness. It may continue to be relatively impotent. What is altered is the meaning of that impotence. It is now an experience of being overcome by an alien and greater power. The Jungians interpret a great deal of myth as expressing this shift of the seat of existence into reflective consciousness and the intrapsychic struggles that ensue.

My thesis is that by the axial period the shift of the seat of existence to the reflective consciousnesss was occurring in influential segments of the community. This led to the progressive rationalizing of reflective consciousness, as well as to its strengthening. Finally, rational consciousness was prepared to assert its full autonomy from, and its power over, the mythical symbolization by which ancient civilization had lived. The power of mythical thinking was broken, and a new structure of existence emerged.

This newness can be seen in the individuality and freedom of axial man. This does not mean that men who had always been individual and free finally came to see this fact about themselves. Instead, it means that individuality and freedom arose. The next pages will be devoted to an attempt to explain the newness of axial existence first as individuality and then as freedom.

Of course, men have always been individuals in some sense. Ontologically speaking, every entity is individual. Furthermore, men have always had an important measure of individual identity through time. In contrast to the higher animals, among which the successive dominant occasions of experience are primarily bound to the present condition of the body and only secondarily constitute a unity through time as they are joined together into a psyche, human experience has always had considerable autonomy. For it, the relation to its own past and future is more determinative than the relation to the changing condition of the body. Ontologically, therefore, not only is each occasion of human experience an individual, just as is each animal experience as well, but also the series of such occasions has a continuity and a cumulative character that constitute it as an individual series.

In primitive man, however, this individuality was located in the unconscious, and although it must be emphasized when we compare human experience with that of animals, it was not what we think of as individuality today. When I think of myself as an individual, I think of that thread of consciousness that I can recall from the past and anticipate in the future and with which I can identify myself. To a large extent my conscious decisions are made on the basis of memories of past conscious experiences and anticipations of future ones. Thus I bind together this sequence into a chain that began with birth and ends with death. As an individual, I am that chain, and I perceive myself as clearly distinguished and sharply separated from all other individuals.

Because the identity by which I am constituted is primarily a unity of conscious experience, this sharp division of myself from all others is real. My conscious relation to my conscious past and future is drastically different from my conscious relation to the consciousness of other individuals. This relation to others is indirect and even inferential rather than immediate and constitutive. Nevertheless, I believe that even for the highly conscious individual there are other relations to other individuals in the unconscious dimensions of experience. Our total experience in each moment is a selective synthesis of the whole world as it gives itself to be experienced. Important elements in that world are the past experiences of the individual in question, but the experiences of other men are also there to be appropriated. One's own past may outweigh the others in importance, but it does not exclude them. Hence, our experience as a whole is far more a social product than we ordinarily realize.

Even axial men sometimes receive dim intuitions of the social character of their experience. They sense a greater immediacy of psychic presence of their fellows than their usual theories can explain. Extrasensory communications of various kinds occasionally enter consciousness to disturb our rationalistic systems based on the supposed primacy of sensory experience. Nevertheless, this dimension of experience is too trivial within our conscious lives to play more than a peripheral role. In the unconscious, on the other hand, its importance is far greater.

This means that when the seat of existence was located in the unconscious, individual identity through time was far less exclusive than it became with the axial shift of center to consciousness. Each moment of human experience was certainly deeply affected by its predecessors in the life of the individual soul, but it was also deeply influenced by the psychic life of other members of the tribe. The unconscious experience of each contributed to the unconscious experience of others in such a way that the group or tribe constituted a unit of psychic life quite inconceivable for axial man.

Consciousness also played an important role in the life of primitive man. But so long as the seat of existence was in the unconscious, the relation of the conscious element of one experience to those of others was mediated by the unconscious. In this situation, the symbolic content of consciousness expressed the unconscious life and thus, primarily, the shared psychic life of the group.

Primitive man understood himself as constituted by his participation in a larger whole, rather than conceiving of the whole as composed of individual men who are the final agents of action, decision, and real individuality. I am suggesting that this understanding corresponded with the reality of his situation. Hence, I am arguing also that the emergence of axial man was not only the emergence of a new understanding of man as individual, but of a new individuality. When the seat of existence shifted effectively to reflective consciousness, a new type of continuity between successive occasions of experience arose as well as a new separation of the individual thus constituted from all other individuals.

We can also describe the appearance of axial man as the emergence of freedom. In one sense, every occasion of experience enjoys some freedom in forming itself into whatever it becomes in its moment of actuality. But it is better not to use the term "freedom" quite so broadly. The great majority of what we ordinarily mean by freedom is absent from subhuman modes of existence. What is present is some element of spontaneity and self-determination, an element that has increasing importance as we ascend the scale of life.

Self-determination is fully characteristic of unconscious experience. That does not mean, of course, that it is the primary factor in such experiences. It only means that the process of self-determination by organizing and synthesizing the data from the past mostly occurs unconsciously. Consciousness is possible at all only after this process has progressed to a very high level. Hence, unconscious self-determination is quantitatively primary, even for the most rational man. But it will be best for us to reserve the term "freedom" for something quite different, something much more distinctive and rare.

Where reflective consciousness occurred, there the self-determination present everywhere played a much larger and wider role. Nevertheless, as long as the symbol system was determined by the unconscious, it did not alter the fundamental character of unconscious self-determination.

With the rationalization of reflective consciousness and the shift of the seat of existence to the rational consciousness, a new element appeared, namely, conscious control of symbolization and, thereby, also of action. In axial man this possible conscious control was extended in principle to the whole gamut of human action and thought. One no longer need do and think just what had been done and thought, and the mythical meanings by which man had lived so long were now problematic rather than simply given. At this point, we can and should speak of human freedom as something of utmost importance and distinctiveness in relation to mere unconscious self-determination. In this very important sense, the appearance of axial man was the emergence of freedom in the world.

In this discussion of both individuality and freedom, I have contrasted only primitive man and axial man. Here the contrast is sharp and clear. But between the tribal consciousness of primitive men and the rise of the axial individual lay many centuries of Neolithic culture and high civilization. This period may be subsumed under the heading of the mythical age, but it is important to recognize the great extent to which it was a time of transition. Rational consciousness played an ever greater role, and we must assume that, for greater or lesser parts of their lives, civilized men found the seat of their existence within this consciousness. Thereby, civilized men found themselves more and more cut off from the unity of group life and thrown into lonely isolation. The experience of individuality and freedom, therefore, was not altogether new in the axial period.

However, it is in the description of axial man and not of civilized man in general that the discussion of freedom and individuality belongs. That which constituted civilized man in his distinction from primitive man did not, in itself, bring with it freedom and individuality. It only provided the conditions within which that gradual development could begin which led to the emergence of axial man. Just as before the rise of civilization, those factors which went into the making of civilized man were already present without gaining adequate expression to alter man's basic situation, so during the course of civilization, those factors arose which went into the making of axial man without transforming the basic character of civilized existence.

Thus we may say that the rise of rational consciousness as an important new factor, which constituted the threshold crossed by civilized man, prepared for the possibility that the seat of existence shift into this consciousness. Where this possibility existed, it undoubtedly was actualized from time to time, and with increasing frequency. This shift in its turn further strengthened the rational consciousness, and finally man was able, from this new seat of existence, to assert conscious control over the whole of consciousness. The effective success of this effort, transforming the whole of existence, is to be found in the first millennium before Christ and is the defining mark of axial man.

I have been speaking as if primitive man, civilized man, and axial man each constituted a single type, recognizing that they shaded off into each other; but we must also recognize that the variations among groups and individuals belonging to each are very great. Yet in the case of the first two, for our purposes, these varieties could be neglected. When we turn to axial man, the situation changes. Here the possible range of diversity is still greater, and some consideration of this diversity is essential to the understanding of our own situation and of Christianity. Hence, the following chapters are discussions of several types of axial existence.

Chapter Six

BUDDHIST EXISTENCE

THE DEVELOPMENT OF AXIAL man out of archaic civilization may have taken place both earlier and more gradually in India than in the other major centers. By the time of Gautama in the sixth century, the development was already complete. Gautama's work must be seen as interaction with and modification of a situation in which axial man already existed.

The earlier stage of this development is expressed in some of the Upanishads, and it may be that already by the ninth century, the axial stage of consciousness had been reached. On the other hand, the Upanishads also include much material of a mythical sort, and the line between the mythical and rational is far from clear. It is possible that the emergence of men dominated in their self-understanding by conscious rationality hardly antedates the sixth century.

The question of dates is a minor one for our purposes. Our major concern is to gain some understanding of the form taken by the axial revolution in India. What fundamental interest determined the categories by which the rational consciousness organized its world? What categories, in fact, structured this world for Indian man?

To gain a basis for understanding the Indian development in its distinctness, it is necessary to risk a few generalizations about the role of religion in archaic civilization. In primitive cultures, there was no such thing as religion as one among the activities and functions of the society. The mythical symbol structure gave meaning to all activities, and thus the whole of life participated in the sacred. Whatever did not participate in the sacred lacked reality and fundamental acceptability. By sharing with the whole tribe in this one reality, men existed primarily as parts of the whole rather than as individuals in voluntary or involuntary association.

But with the rise of civilization, as we have seen, increasingly important areas of life came to be governed by an alternate symbol system. The conditions of civilized life forced on man a greater degree of separateness from the community. Participation in the larger whole became not so much the given reality as something hungered for. Man experienced himself as estranged from unity and wholeness and thrown into a world in which individual existence was a burden. In this situation, religion functioned in two major ways. It continued to function in continuity with the mythical symbol systems of the past, as the foundation of meaning and communal unity and the magical means of obtaining desired goods. But now it began to function also as the means for overcoming the sense of isolation and separateness that civilization brought with it. Of course, these functions can be separated sharply only from a later perspective. Yet we can identify in ancient civilizations the beginnings of a ministry to the felt needs of individuals alongside the communal celebrations and magic rites.

In India, the emerging conscious rationality focused its attention on interpreting the traditional religious activities in terms of the increasingly insistent needs of individuals to find freedom from the suffering of isolation and estrangement. Axial man emerged in the process of the religious quest itself. The victory of rational reflection occurred in the struggle to find freedom from the pain and suffering of individualization and separateness.

For almost the whole of Indian thought, the pain of the human situation was accentuated by the view that present existence is only a small part of the whole. That is, one did not think of birth and death as the beginning and ending of experience. Rather, they were only transitions from one state of being to another. This conviction of immortality, far from comforting and reassuring the suffering individual, indicated to him that even in death he could not escape the burden and terror of existence.

It is difficult for us to understand just what is involved in this ancient doctrine of transmigration. Probably it antedated the emergence of that kind of individuality treated in the last chapter. In its primitive form, it did not mean that the reflective individual conceived of himself as having had innumerable prior lives and as destined for many future ones. Rather, it reflected a less individualized understanding of existence, in which what persisted were impersonal processes that gained particularized expression in human experience. Where a heightened sense of individuality emerged in the axial period, the problem was changed, but it is significant that the vision of beginninglessness and of endlessness constituted the context of thought for the axial thinkers of India. The meaning and character of this endlessness was interpreted and reinterpreted, but rarely did there emerge the clear sense of radical beginning with physical birth and radical ending with physical death that the Western mind often mistakenly identifies with universal common sense.

Most Indian thinkers, in their passionate quest for release from the unbearable situation in which the individual found himself, also shared a common assumption that the experience of isolation and estrangement pointed to a reality other than that which is immediately and obviously given. The sheer phenomenal flux and the sheer givenness of separate existence were rationally unintelligible as well as existentially unendurable. The task of thought was so to penetrate through this phenomenal world that man could find his way to reality itself.

Thus in India, the quest for individual salvation from the pain of sheer individuality was immediately and inextricably involved with the ontological or metaphysical question as to the real. Far earlier than in the West, many of the major possible answers to this question were formulated with profound sophistication and insight. The fact that the metaphysical quest was inseparable from the existential one meant that each answer to the former was also a religious movement or school. In a purely schematic way, we can note some of the varieties of Indian thought and their diverse implications for the quest for release or salvation.

The two fundamental metaphysical possibilities considered by the Indian thinkers were pluralism and monism. Pluralism is the view that ultimate reality is composed of numerous monads, that is, that the whole of reality is constituted by the addition of its parts. Monism is the view that the appearance of multiplicity is finally an error, that reality is finally one, and that all diversity must be seen in the light of that truth. We can consider briefly the kinds of consequences that were drawn from these fundamental convictions.[14]

The chief pluralistic doctrines were Jaina and Sankhya. In the Jaina view, all monads were material entities, but they differ from each other greatly in their intrinsic heaviness or darkness. The life monad, that which man knew as himself, was by nature the most ethereal form of matter and belonged at the top of the universe. But the accumulated results of its actions had contaminated it with the weight and darkness of the grosser monads. Man was called to release himself from this contamination and involvement. By cutting himself off from those activities that increased his involvement in the world and by worship, he could gradually free himself and rise toward his rightful place. He did not, in such a process, cease to be an ontological individual, but he was freed from all those properties which distinguished him from other individuals in any way except numerically.

In the Sankhya view, the life monads were differentiated more radically from the world of things. There was something more like a dualism of mind and matter, or of the psychic and physical. The difference was understood as such that there could be no actual ontological contamination or involvement of the life monads in the material sphere. In reality, they remained quite free and pure. The problem was that this reality was concealed from the busy ego. It believed itself to be constantly affected by all the changing world of things. The task was to still the restless activity of the mind so that the true self could become visible in its absolute imperturbability. When man recognized himself thus for what he was, wholly beyond the sphere of change and suffering, he experienced reality and was released from the illusion of actual participation in change and suffering. He did not cease to be an individual monad, numerically distinct from all other monads. But again, as in the Jaina view, all that appeared to distinguish one individual from another qualitatively was stripped away. In the fulfilled state, there was release from all

---

[14] For the treatment of Jaina, Sankhya, and Vedanta, I am largely indebted to Heinrich Zimmer, *Philosophies of India* (Meridian Books, Inc., 1956).

consciousness of separateness and, indeed, from consciousness as such.

The difference between these two views was that for the Jaina the involvement of the life monads in the world was real, whereas for the Sankhya it was an illusion. This difference had as its concomitant some difference in the way of seeking release. For the Jaina, the task was that of real purification, requiring definite modes of action and abstinence from action. For the Sankhya, what was required was an intellectual and existential freeing from error. Reflection and psychic discipline had their importance for the Jaina, and action and abstinence from action had their importance for the Sankhya, but the development of particular psychic disciplines was especially associated with Sankhya, whereas the attempt to avoid totally any destruction of life was a peculiar mark of Jaina.

In sharp ontological contrast to these pluralistic philosophies was Vedanta. Vedanta insisted that ultimately all reality was one and that all plurality was mere appearance. This applied, of course, to the outer world. The variety of sense experience was only the variety of ways in which the one metaphysical reality, Brahman, presented itself superficially to men. But much more important, the true self of every man, Atman, was also one with Brahman. We must pause briefly to consider what this meant — that Brahman and Atman were one.

Atman was not the conscious ego of axial man nor the teeming unconscious experience out of which this arose. In the Vedanta analysis, both conscious and unconscious were phenomenal and transitory expressions of an underlying subject, the ultimate self. But this ultimate self turned out upon analysis not in fact to be characterized by the variegated experience of the psyche. It was the subject of all that experience, but in its own nature it was unaffected by it. The subject of change did not itself change. Thus, like the life monads of Sankhya, it was qualitatively undifferentiated. But Vedanta went farther. The ultimate undifferentiated subject of a man's experience, that is, his self, could not be other than the ultimate undifferentiated subject of any other man's experience or, indeed, Brahman itself, the one unchanging subject of all change. Thus man's true self, in distinction from his apparent self, was that one unchanging reality that expressed itself in all the appearance of change.

The religious implications of Vedantist monism were not very different from those of Sankhya pluralism. For Vedanta, like Sankhya, the problem was not *real* contamination or separateness or evil, but the misleading appearance from which true knowledge could free men. To gain this true knowledge could not be merely a matter of rational assent to the doctrine that Atman is Brahman. It must be, also, progressive experiential realization of this unity. For this purpose, psychic disciplines like those associated with Sankhya were appropriate.

In the account of these Indian philosophies, it has been necessary to introduce a term heretofore avoided — the term "self." In our Western usage, it is tempting to identify the self with the seat of existence as defined in the preceding chapter. For us, the self is the center from which our conscious experience is organized. However, this identification cannot be made in a comparative study such as this one.

The seat of existence of Hindu man, no less than of Western man, was in the rational consciousness, and he recognized the natural tendency to identify this with his self. But precisely this tendency is what he rejected, and this in diverse ways. Atman, which is translated as "self," had connotations of ultimacy and self-identity that did not fit the seat of existence. The Indian recognized, as few Westerners have done before modern times, how much of the psychic life is organized around centers largely independent of the seat of existence. Hence, he sought to overcome the habit of self-identification with the seat of existence and to discover the true self as something quite different. Such an undertaking required a type of awareness of the psychic processes rarely attained in the West. In the West, the identification of the self with the seat of existence has been virtually unquestioned until recent times, although many of the connotations of the Indian Atman have confusedly been associated with it.

The most important individual figure to appear in the axial period of Indian history was Gautama Buddha. His focus of interest, like that of the schools discussed above, was release or salvation from the endless and meaningless chain of being. But his reflection was, in some respects, more radical than the others. The transition from archaic to axial modes of thought had occurred in India without a sharp break. Metaphysical reflection had continued to employ categories derived from the mythical background and context of thought. Metaphysics and myth interpenetrated each other and lived comfortably in mutual tolerance. Down to the present day, the Indian thinkers, who employ the most lucid rationality in their own reflection, often defend the appropriateness of religious practices on the part of the masses that have almost unbroken continuity with the mythical past. Since axial man had appeared in India without demanding any radical break with the past, he left the masses largely undisturbed in their preaxial state.

Buddhism, in contrast, insisted on a much more drastic departure from the past. Any conceptuality by which man tried to understand ultimate reality was, it was convinced, tainted and distorting.[15] The very idea of a "reality" in contradistinction to the appearance of things represented for it a false conceptuality. Brahman was not "real" and Atman was not "real." "Reality" as such was a null class; it was a part of that mythical mentality that was only partly rationalized in the metaphysical schools. The whole speculative thrust of these schools was, from the Buddhist point of view, misguided or unenlightened, for the very good reason that its questions were meaningless. When one was truly enlightened, one turned one's attention away from the mythical-metaphysical to the practical. Conversely, the safest path to enlightenment was also to be found in the practical.

By the practical, of course, Buddhism did not mean what we moderns might mean, namely, the production of goods and the improvement of socioeconomic conditions. It meant, rather, the identification and practice of that way of life which led to freedom from anxiety and suffering and the achievement of serenity in complete independence of outward experience. Such serenity in its ultimate form involved the transcendence of any concern for self and, hence, of all selfhood. But since such serenity did not depend on grasping the

[15] So that distinctions may be clearly seen, the Buddhist view is presented in its opposition to the Hindu schools. Gautama himself did not teach in this way.

truth of some metaphysical formula, the road to its attainment lay in moderation and acceptance of things as they were rather than in ascetic discipline and paranormal experience.

The denial of the reality of the self, Atman, may seem to be itself a metaphysical doctrine requiring the attainment of a special state of mind for its acceptance. In a broad sense of "metaphysical," this is true. But we must remember that the term "metaphysical" even today has connotations derived from the experience of the sacred and from myth. That is, metaphysical seems, in many ears, to point to an "eminent" reality transcending the obvious and mundane world of commonplace experience. The metaphysical is thought of as that which is above or beyond the transiency of the merely temporal. Atman certainly had these connotations in most Indian thought. The reality of Atman was eminent in relation to the merely phenomenal, apparent world, including the ego and its normal consciousness. In part, this eminence consisted in its freedom from change and decay. In Vedanta, this eminence was fully articulated in the doctrine that this Atman was really Brahman itself, the one, ultimate, supersensible, holy reality.

The denial of Atman, therefore, on the part of Buddhism was not some strange metaphysical doctrine to the effect that the flow of experience did not occur or that there was no seat of existence in human experiences. It was, rather, the denial that there was some other dimension of reality in comparison with which this one was mere appearance or illusion.

If there was no reality beyond the successive moments of experience, then man's self-understanding as a permanent subject enjoying adventures through time was an illusion. Whatever unity the successive experiences had must be a function of these experiences themselves. Since this unity could not be caused by either past or future experiences, the agent and ground of unity through time was seen to be the present occasion of experience. To the extent to which in each moment a man believed himself to be identical with his past and future, that identity persisted. With it, there continued regret and anxiety and, above all, desire. To the extent that through enlightenment a man recognized the unreality of this relation, the present moment of experience was, in fact, freed from it and from the concomitant emotions. Man thus could achieve serenity in a non-temporal moment.[16]

A similar analysis applies to the Buddhist understanding of the environment. Buddhism did not deny the reality of the environing world, but it believed that the world as given in the ordinary reflective consciousness was a product of the concepts, hopes, fears, and desires of man. In this way, the Buddhist believed, the world was falsely perceived as substantial, causal, and filled with meanings for human existence. Enlightenment reduced the environment to mere momentary congeries of elements lacking all significance for human existence. In this way, the emotional life could be disengaged from attachment to and involvement in the world.[17]

This process can be explained in the categories by which this book is organized. In these terms, Buddhism accepted the world as given in the reflective consciousness as real. But we have seen that the world, in relationship to which we actually live, is a significantly ordered

[16] From my Whiteheadian viewpoint, Buddhism seems subtly to have exaggerated the capacity of an actual occasion of human experience to determine its own relation to its predecessors. Buddhism attributed true causality to the prehending occasion only, holding that it alone is ultimately responsible for how it prehends its predecessors. This doctrine led to the theoretical ideal of an occasion that suspends such prehensions altogether. Whitehead holds that the decisions of the past occasions inescapably play a causally efficacious role in setting the limits of the present occasion. This means that the present occasion *must* take account of past occasions and reenact aspects of them. This does not deny the possibility of a very different relation to this past from that which is normal to us. Nevertheless, from the Whiteheadian perspective, the ideal of the timeless moment is an illusion.

[17] Once again, despite the far-reaching similarities between Whitehead's ontology and Buddhism, a Whiteheadian must record his judgment that Buddhism is involved in a subtle illusion similar to that of much Western philosophy. By concentrating on experience in the mode of presentational immediacy, Buddhism is led to empty the environing world of real significance for human existence. It correctly shows that in *this* mode the supposed causality and the human meanings that are found are humanly projected. This process of projection may be subjected to human control. However, Buddhism does not finally acknowledge the inescapable causal efficacy of the past, an efficacy only partly subject to the control of the present occasion of human experience. This efficacy means that the environment has real significance for human existence, which may or may not correlate closely with projected meanings.

world This significant ordering is partly by signals and partly by symbols. It is guided largely by organic needs and by conscious and unconscious desires.

The Buddhist correctly saw that man's emotional involvement with his world is a function of this significant ordering and that this significant ordering is man's own work. Destitute of such ordering, the phenomenal environment is simply what it is, barren of reference to past or future. Recognizing this, the Buddhist learned to suspend or interrupt his habits of significant ordering.

The overcoming of self-identity through time can also be described in the categories developed in the preceding chapters. The final ontological individual is the actual momentary occasion of experience, in this case, of human experience. Each occasion is influenced by many factors, only one of which is the group of preceding occasions of human experience that conjointly with successor occasions constitutes the human soul from birth to death.

Among primitive peoples, this relationship to previous and successor human occasions had not attained such decisive prominence as to constitute human individuality in the full sense. With the rise of civilization, however, human identity through time became much more marked, and by the axial period it was fully established.

Where the sense of identity was strongly developed, the sense of isolation was an inevitable concomitant. We have already seen how important a role this played in ancient religion and in axial thinking in India. Concomitantly, there arose an acute problem for reflection, a problem we have still not solved.

On the one hand, we experience an overpowering sense of identity through time. On the other hand, the actual experiences that give the content to this one identical selfhood are constantly changing. If we trust the sense of identity, we seem driven to regard the changing experiences as nonessential to our ultimate selfhood. In their different ways, Jaina and Sankhya took this road. If we strip that which constitutes our identity of all particularity, as these philosophies did and had to do, if they were to display the identity as absolute, then there is nothing left by which to distinguish one individual from another. Vedanta drew the reasonable conclusion of monism.

In none of these movements was the identity through time especially prized. It was the given fact, not even deeply affected by birth or death, in terms of which man constituted a problem for himself. If this sheer identity could be freed from its involvement in the phenomenal and transitory world, then there could be peace, and this was the common goal of all the philosophical schools of India.

But despite the immense self-evidence of self-identity through time for all civilized peoples, we have seen that it is not an ontological necessity. The primacy of our relation to past and future occasions of our own experience in relation to other experiences is not absolute. Individual identity through time is a matter of degree. Hence, it may be that the quest for an absolutely self-identical subject of change is fruitless. Perhaps what man must realize instead is that each moment of experience is simply what it is. Perhaps the marked individuality that characterizes civilized man is just what must be overcome. Perhaps it is constituted by fears and hopes and desires, and perhaps it is just these things which bind man to the endless and meaningless chain of existence from which he needs to be freed. This, I take it, was the distinctive direction of much Buddhist thought.

A central thesis of this book is that the diversities among cultures are not simply in their leading ideas but also in the structures of existence they embody and express. Hence, the remainder of this chapter is devoted to a more direct statement as to how these Indian views of man's situation express and encourage peculiar structures of existence.

Among the Indians, as among all axial peoples, the reflective consciousness gained autonomy from the unconscious and was effectively rationalized. The seat of existence established itself in this rational consciousness, and from this center it overcame and reinterpreted its mythical heritage. This resulted in the emergence of freedom and individuality, as explained in the last chapter. However, the Indian was not satisfied with this general axial structure of existence and struggled against it. He rejected the new axial existence because of its isolation and suffering. Nevertheless, he participated too fully in it to seek release in a return to mythical existence.

The Hindu attempted to overcome his self-identification with his rational consciousness by objectifying that consciousness in its totality and thus transcending it and dissociating himself from it. What this meant for the structure of existence is far clearer in its negative than in its positive meaning. Negatively, it meant that whatever aspect of conscious or unconscious experience could be conceptualized or objectified was distinguished as other than, alien from, and, finally, even indifferent to the self. Although this did not lead to a return to the dominance of the unconscious, it did prevent the new seat of existence in consciousness from entering upon any further develop·ment. Because the seat of existence in each moment negated itself, its consciousness of itself as continuing through time, as responsibly purposing, willing, and controlling, was constantly undermined.

That this led to positive psychic states, which are to Western eyes both strange and remarkable, is clear. That it actually led to the realization of an undifferentiated and unindividualized self is much more questionable. This would be possible only on the assumption of the reality of such a metaphysical entity, and on this point Buddhist skepticism has much justification. From the point of view of the assumptions with which this whole analysis proceeds, the structure of existence to which Buddhism led is much more fully intelligible than the Hindu goal. My view, like that of many Buddhists, is that the ultimate ontological individual is a momentary occasion of experience. Such occasions came to be organized into a linear succession characterized by continuity and cumulation. When the whole of consciousness has its center within consciousness, axial individuality emerges. This center identifies itself with the comparable centers in past and future dominant occasions in the organism. But since this self-identity through time is not ontologically given, it can also be destroyed without destroying the succession of occasions themselves.

Axial individuality could be overcome by rejecting consciousness in favor of unconsciousness and thus relapsing into a preaxial state, but it could also be removed — or rendered ineffectual — by dissociation of each momentary occasion from its connection with its predecessors and successors. Since the connection is constituted for consciousness by memory and anticipation, the unity through time could in principle be broken by cessation of memory and anticipation, or by viewing one's own past and future in just the way one views any other past and future.

It must be emphasized that the past and future from which each occasion was thus dissociated was not only the relatively remote past and future, temporally separated from the present by minutes, but also the immediate past and future, only a second or less away. When one ceased in each moment to identify oneself with these predecessor and successor occasions, the conscious connection between these occasions was trivialized and axial individuality was overcome. Identity through time was relegated to the unconscious, while the seat of existence remained in consciousness. Thus at the level of full conscious control, the individuality produced by consciousness was destroyed. With it were removed desire and anxiety, and these were replaced by serenity, disinterestedness, and perfect unconcern.

Chapter Seven

HOMERIC EXISTENCE

IN EARLIER CHAPTERS we have distinguished between the receptive consciousness, the consciousness organized in terms of signals, and the symbolically ordered or reflective consciousness. In Chapters Four and Five, we traced the progressive rationalization of the reflective consciousness. This rationalization is a process of replacing the mythical symbols provided by the unconscious with others derived from nonreflective consciousness.

In general, the rationalization of reflective consciousness proceeded through its close association with the intelligent interpretation of signals. Symbols that were projected on the environment were checked against observed relations in that environment. The resulting modification of the symbols served the practical end of better adaptation to, and control over, the environment.

This account of the emergence of rational consciousness has omitted reference to receptive consciousness. This is because it was those aspects of experience which were already significantly organized in terms of signals which could be most readily employed to check and modify unconscious symbolization. However, along with the emergence of the rational consciousness, there arose heightened ability also to attend to the content of receptive awareness. This attending extended the possibility of checking and reforming the symbolization by which the whole of experience had been unconsciously organized.

An element of objectification or distancing is present in all rationalization of the reflective consciousness. The whole process involves the distinguishing of the internal from the external and the allowing to the external of its autonomous existence. The forms of thought are conformed to the relations actually observed in the external world. However, this distancing of the object from the subject is generally for the sake of practical purposes.

In addition to such practical distancing of objects, there is a more radical form in which the object is accorded its freedom also from the interests of the subject. This we can call aesthetic distancing. In aesthetic distancing, the content of the receptive consciousness plays the primary role, although significantly organized experience can also be objectified in this way. Once the psychic act of distancing is performed, the subject is open to being formed by what is given in the object. Thus in this case as well, the mythical symbolization gives way to forms determined by objective reality.

It would be foolish to suggest that the psychic act of aesthetic distancing occurred for the first time among the Greeks. Here, as everywhere, we must assume gradual development of the new rather than sudden emergence. Nevertheless, it seems that only among the Greeks did the habit of aesthetic distancing attain sufficient strength or stability to play a dominant role in the formation of the basic structures of human existence.

All distancing involves the suspension of our deep-seated habit of projecting symbols on the world. It does not, thereby, bring about the cessation of the unconscious processes in which these symbols are produced. Hence, alongside the appreciation of the beauty of the world made possible by aesthetic distancing, the Greek experienced the products of his unconscious activities as numinous and threatening powers.

The unique psychic act by which the Greeks entered axial existence was an aesthetic projection of the gods by which Olympian religion was brought into being. Such an aesthetic *projection* is a very different phenomenon from aesthetic distancing, for it is a projection of a content not given to receptive consciousness. Yet, it is also radically different from the type of projection characteristic of mythical existence, because it aesthetically orders the products of unconscious processes into an aesthetically distanced world.

Mythical projection involves the symbolization of elements given in unreflective experience in forms determined by unconscious processes. Thus, from the point of view of the rational consciousness, it distorts the sensuously given world. *Aesthetic* projection treats the products of unconscious processes as if they were of the same order as that which is given in receptive awareness. It thus introduces these symbols into the sensuously given world, but without confusing them with any other entities in that world. In this way, their power to distort experience of that world is broken. Indeed by aesthetic projection of the gods, the Greeks subordinated mythical meanings to the rational consciousness. The gods were conceived as visual objects having excellence in themselves, an excellence that inspired interest and admiration rather than numinous terror or the expectation of interference in the practical affairs of life.

These gods had existed among the Greeks, as among all primitive and archaic peoples, as numinous products of unconscious processes. The stories and rituals in which they were apprehended were the language of a consciousness enslaved to these unconscious meanings. The Indian thinkers of the axial period simply denied or relativized these deities. The Greeks, however, because they had aesthetically projected the gods, could treat the myths as if they were the bearers of intelligible meanings. This does not mean that they approached the myths as moderns, believing only what accorded with some kind of evidence, or seeking the kernel of existential truth in the supernaturalistic husk. But they did undertake to impose an intelligible order upon the myths, which were thus enabled to become a part of the conscious life rather than a pervasive threat to its autonomy and dominance. In this way arose the mythological in distinction from the mythical.

The process by which the gods, as representatives of the powers of the unconscious, were domesticated by the rational consciousness of the Greeks can be traced through a period of centuries. It was, however, in the work of Homer that the Greeks themselves saw the Bible of their Olympian religion. In these writings, the mysterious and fearful gods were transformed into idealized persons, not without their all-too-human foibles, but just for that reason understandable and freed from dread. Further, they were provided an intelligible order in their relation with one another. These idealized men and women were projected to a distance and endowed with immortality and superhuman power. They no longer constituted a pervasive aspect of the total experience of the world.

Because of the normative importance of Homer for pre-Socratic Greek culture, the distinctive structure of existence that arose in this culture can be called "Homeric existence." It is important to recognize that the term "Homeric culture" is elsewhere more often used to refer to the pre-Dorian civilization reflected in the Homeric epics, a civilization which, in terms of the language here employed, was "pre-Homeric." In this book, "Homeric culture" refers to that culture made possible by the aesthetic distancing unconsciously accomplished in the Homeric epics. This is the period in which the Olympian gods and such myths as those associated with the Trojan War were taken seriously, provided the major material for sculptors and poets, and profoundly influenced the vision of reality. Its last great literary expressions were in Aeschylus and Sophocles. In the fifth century before Christ are to be found both the climax of this culture and its erosion by the Sophists and Euripides as well as the rise of Socratic existence. There is a rich development from Homer to the tragedians, and the historians and pre-Socratic philosophers provide other important variations. It might be better to interpret the period in terms of several threshold crossings and, hence, of several structures of existence. However, I am attempting to present the whole culture in terms of fundamental and unifying factors capable of explaining also its great variety and internal development.

Chief among these unifying factors was the aesthetic objectification that has been emphasized above. Not only sensory experience and the numinous products of the unconscious, but also the emotions and passions were distanced in this way. But what was distanced could not exhaust the content of existence. Hence, the objectified gods stood in an ambiguous relation to that other primal religious reality that represented the apportionment to each entity of its lot or place. As the ultimate ground of order in nature and human life, *moira* was, at times, almost regarded as a function of the will of Zeus. But this was not quite possible. The ground of order could not be reduced to a function of one entity within the aesthetically ordered world. The gods, too, had their portions, which, however great, implied also their limits. Thus *moira* was also fate, an inevitability of outcome against which man struggled in vain and which the gods themselves were unable to deflect. As that which was ordained beyond all willing and all comprehension, *moira* was also a darkness surrounding the radiant, but all too narrow, world of consciousness.

For and within Homeric existence, *moira* functioned as a limit. But this existence as a whole was challenged and threatened in the form of Dionysianism. In Homeric existence, the dominance of the unconscious over the conscious was broken by the aesthetic ordering of its products. But the exclusion of unconscious symbolization from consciousness did not destroy the power of the unconscious. It only estranged it. In its estranged state it took upon itself new forms and expressed itself in new ways. Dionysianism was in continuity with primitive and antique religions, but the dominance of the Homeric culture forced upon it a new character and a new role. A discussion of this important aspect of the Greek experience is not possible in this chapter, where attention is focused on Homeric existence as the original form of axial existence in Greece. Nevertheless, it is important to recognize that what was excluded in Homeric existence forced itself on the attention of Homeric man as a profound threat and that, to a considerable extent, the Greek tragedy was the attempt, almost successful, to include the Dionysian powers within the beauty and order of the Homeric world. In this it went far beyond the Homeric epics and represents the maturest expression of Homeric existence.

The act of aesthetic distancing is not only one of introducing separation but also one of attending to form. Furthermore, this distancing has its clearest and easiest exemplification in visual experience, and it was in this dimension that the Greeks projected and objectified their gods. Alongside power and immortality, and to some extent superseding them as time went by, their most striking attribute was beauty of physical form. At least in the work of the sculptors who celebrated the Homeric deities, perfection of visible form became the all-consuming concern. Since, in the initial act of distancing, the gods were portrayed as idealized men and women, the beauty celebrated by the Greeks was ever the beauty of the human body. A beautiful man was hardly to be distinguished from a god either in his own excellence or in the admiration he excited. Hence, rational man no longer stood before a mysterious and foreign reality, in front of which he must grovel and to which he must sacrifice his distinctively human aspirations. Man's consciousness moved into the center of a stage cleared of unconscious mythical power.

Both the sensitivity to visual form and the glorification of the human are also attested by the Greek temple. It was the most humanistic of cultic buildings. What this means can best be indicated by contrast. The dimensions of the Greek temple did not inspire awe and the sense of mystery. The temple did not soar toward the heavens or dwarf the beholder into insignificance. It did not embody the powerful symbolism of the unconscious or point to some fulfillment of man in relation to a superhuman state. Rather, the Greek temple embodied just those formal values which reason could apprehend. It achieved balance and proportion, an aesthetically pleasing form that neither thrilled nor frightened. It encouraged the viewer to keep his distance, a distance from which he could enjoy the perfection of intelligible beauty.

In other words, the Greek temple helped the human observer to organize his world in terms of objective forms, rather than in terms of subconscious forces or aspiration for some superhuman state. It belonged, with the Homeric gods it honored, to the sphere of human beauty. Where the gods were displayed in relief and sculpture, they only served further to idealize the beauty of man himself, not to overawe him or drive him into shame for his merely human condition.

The aesthetic projection of the gods made possible, in its turn, a still greater freedom in the aesthetic distancing of the real environment. It thereby provided a context in which the capacity for careful and objective observation of the natural world could make great advances. Even more important, the dispassionate creation and admiration of harmonious forms, so remarkably exemplified in Greek sculpture and architecture, provided a congenial environment for investigation of the nature of form as such. The Greek mind, liberated from myth, was open to mathematical inquiries far transcending the practically oriented and magically conceived mathematics of the ancient civilizations. Its greatest development was in the study of space, and, for the Greeks, a certain spatiality always clung to the idea of number and quantity. This is not surprising when we consider how closely the act of distancing was bound up with visual experience, and how a detached and critical interest in form depended on this act of distancing.

In their reflection on forms, the Greeks made two major discoveries. They found that laws of form, quantitatively conceived, are capable of absolute demonstration and universalization. They found also that such qualitative forms as musical tones correlate with quantitative measures and can be expressed as functions of mathematical laws. With those two discoveries the Greeks were launched into the development of natural science and philosophy. Their sustained and brilliant speculations both presupposed and furthered their extraordinary capacity for distancing the total environment, especially as it was given in vision. Both the careful observation of nature and the bold speculative generalizations with which this was combined expressed a rare freedom from the practical concerns of life as well as from the mythical mentality.

The process of distancing went even farther. The Greeks not only reasoned with extraordinary clarity and daring, but they also inquired into the forms of reasoning itself. These forms, too, they objectified and reduced to order, thus founding the discipline of logic. They considered the relation of the forms embodied in reason and the forms embodied in nature, and thus further extended their philosophical speculations far beyond the range of philosophy of nature.

In summary, Homeric man emerged into axial existence by the psychic acts of the aesthetic distancing of the environment and the aesthetic projection of the gods — psychic acts bound up almost inextricably with vision and the forms given in vision. These two acts were mutually interdependent. Only where the world was aesthetically distanced could the gods be aesthetically projected, and only where the mythical power of the gods was broken by such a projection could man be really free to enjoy his aesthetically distanced environment. Thus the foundation of Greek culture was aesthetic, specifically the aestheticizing of mythical meanings. Within this context, the rational consciousness could pursue its inquiry into forms in geometry, science, and logic.

Our major concern is not to understand the many achievements of the Greeks in art, mathematics, science, and philosophy, but rather to understand the structure of Homeric existence. To approach this question more closely, we must consider briefly the understanding of man expressed in Homeric culture.

I have emphasized that the first stage in the act of distancing was the visual one. The objects of vision were observed apart from their relation to the preexisting emotions, practical needs, and mythical meanings of the observer. They were allowed to present themselves as forms. In Olympian religion, man was understood, presented, and honored in the context of such an act of distancing. In the first instance, this meant that the aesthetic quality of the human body, both male and female, played a role in Greek culture hardly paralleled elsewhere. Probably no other people have been able to celebrate the excellence of form of the naked body in such remarkable separation from sexual interests. But more important, men were presented to the hearer of the poetry or to the viewer of the play objectively — as they would appear to a dispassionate observer. One saw the situation in which they were fated to act, one observed the quality and character of their acts, and one watched as the interaction of the situation and act moved to its inevitable end. The reality of a man was presented as essentially public. It was what it showed itself as being to others.

The Homeric ideal of excellence is to be seen in the context of this understanding of man arising through the act of aesthetic distancing. Excellence was not moral in any usual sense of that term. The heroes were admired for their passion, their forcefulness, their wisdom, their uncompromising insistence on their own dignity, rather than for unselfish service of others, conformity to moral law, or inner purity. These categories scarcely came into play. When something like moral judgment did occur, it had to do with the keeping or breaking of ancient taboos, rather than with the demands of a rationalized morality. Men suffered for breaking these taboos quite apart from the question as to whether they had any choice in the matter. Indeed, they were all the more to be admired because they dared to break the taboos. The taboos were part of the given situation within which greatness had to assert itself. They did not stand in judgment on that greatness.

Despite its love of life and admiration of excellence, the Homeric vision was deeply tragic. Excellence was its own reward, but for his self-assertion man must pay a price. Precisely those whom the Greeks most admired were those who were brought to a terrible destruction by their own excellence. The Greeks knew that the dark and mysterious powers pushed aside by their aesthetic vision of the world remained undestroyed. Sophocles finally portrayed a greatness of such superhuman stature that it was vindicated by the gods themselves, but only after a lifetime of suffering. Aeschylus, in his great trilogy, concluded with a vision of a transformation of the dark powers into supporters of the rational life of the city-state. But in the *Bacchae* of Euripides, we see that the problem was far from solved, that the brilliant achievement of aesthetic reason remained fragile and brittle before the overpowering forces of the unconscious.

In the face of the almost inevitable destruction to which greatness of human self-assertion was seen to lead, there was a second ideal. This ideal received its clearest expression in the choruses of the tragedies. This was the ideal of moderation. The heroes were destroyed, because they refused to conform to the limits that were written into the human situation. They insisted on constituting their own excellence through unlimited willing and acting. The reasonable man, seeing this, might be struck with admiration, but he himself steered another course. He sought to find commonly accepted patterns of behavior, to avoid becoming conspicuous, to observe the taboos, and to bend before the pressure of events so that he would not be broken.

The ideal of moderation was not more "moral" in our usual sense than was heroism. One pursued one's ends with moderation not in order that, thereby, the greater good might be served or so as to sacrifice one's own interests to one's neighbor. One strove for moderation in order to avoid the offense of greatness, in order to escape the tragic consequences of high nobility. The life of moderation respected the taboos, not because one supposed that there was some intrinsic rightness about them, but because one knew that there was danger in their violation.

Homeric man lacked the self-awareness of the Indian sages. These latter knew themselves as subjects and developed intricate analyses of their psychic states and of the interrelation of their introspectively given subjectivity with bodily states. Homeric man understood man as he was given from without through sense experience and especially in vision. Self-awareness could mean only awareness of himself as he appeared to others, rather than as immediately and privately given to himself. Hence, we can find little direct description of the psychic states as such.

What is common to all axial peoples is that the seat of existence shifted from the unconscious to the reflective consciousness, and that, thereby, the reflective consciousness ceased to be bound by the mythical meanings of the unconscious. In being freed from these meanings, it became open to being restructured by the forms given in unreflective consciousness and by principles internal to itself — that is, it became rationalized.

But despite this common structural character, the axial cultures express different structures of existence. To understand what is peculiar to the Buddhist structure of existence, it was necessary to concentrate attention on the relation of each dominant occasion of human experience to the predecessor and successor occasion together with which it constituted a soul. To understand the Homeric structure of existence, on the other hand, we must reflect especially on the subject-object structure of experience, and the ways in which consciousness forms itself in relation to it.

All experience, conscious and unconscious, has ontologically a subject-object structure. The diversity lies in the respective roles of subject and object and in the aspects of this structure that enter consciousness. In mythical existence, the separateness of subject and object was not recognized in experience. There was a flow of symbolically ordered material in which subjective and objective contributions were bound together. There was no clear consciousness of subject as subject or of object as object.

Among the Indian sages, in contrast, there developed an extraordinary understanding of the subject as subject. The psychic processes, which were the content of conscious and unconscious experience, became for them also the objects of awareness, and these were, to an astonishing degree, thereby subjected to conscious control.

Homeric man was incapable of any such understanding of his own psychic processes. For him the object of conscious experience — and he knew of no other kind of experience — was primordially the sensuously given world. Insofar as other entities could be acknowledged at all, they must be assimilated to this world or objectified in analogy with it. For him, as for mythical man, there was no experienced duality of subject and object. But whereas for mythical man the unity of subject and object was one in which the objective was subordinated to the subjective, for Homeric man the subjective was subordinated to the objective. His experienced reality was constituted by the objective pole of experience. Man's own reality to himself, insofar as it could be consciously conceived, was as an actual or possible part of this objective pole of experience.

The dominance of consciousness by its objective pole cut it off from most of the unconscious life of the psyche. Consciousness was dissociated not only from mythical symbols but even from the emotions and passions. These too were perceived as quasi-objective entities. The primacy of sensory objects for consciousness meant that even the most subjective aspects of experience could only enter consciousness as clothed in a comparable objectivity.

The consciousness expressed in the work of the scientist-philosophers embodied a new factor. Their world, too, was initially that of the sensory flux in which vision played the primary role. But with them the activity of abstraction, generalization, and inference came into its own. Here, too, consciousness functioned as conformation to the given as much as, or more than, as a constructive agent, for reasoning was discovery of what was there in the forms rather than a creative act. But the processes of reason opened up a new world beyond that of sensation, a world free from the curse of decay and death, a world in which consciousness came alive in a new way. The dominant object of reflective consciousness ceased to be the flow of sense experience and became, instead, the unchanging forms. Correlatively, the dominant factor within consciousness ceased to be sensuous perception and became, instead, the activity of reason.

Furthermore, a consciousness dominated by reason could achieve a measure of indirect self-awareness denied a consciousness dominated by sensation. Reason objectified itself and attempted to understand itself. However, such logical or metaphysical inquiries into reason did not imply the direct self-awareness of the conscious soul in the sense earlier attained by the Indians. Among the Greek scientist-philosophers, individual consciousness identified itself with reason and then objectified this as an impersonal and universal reality.

We can conclude this chapter by calling attention again to the profound contrast of the existence of Homeric man and Indian man. For Indian man, sense experience was the most superficial and illusory aspect of the soul's life, whereas it constituted the very selfhood of man in Homer's world. Rational activity of the sort so prized by the Greek philosophers could be, for the Indian, at best one factor in the total life of the soul alongside others of equal or greater centrality. Much that the Indian recognized as an integral part of the soul remained for Homeric man something foreign. But from his far more limited base, it was the achievement of Homeric man to find and create a world of harmonious order.

Chapter Eight

SOCRATIC EXISTENCE

ALONGSIDE AND DEPENDENT ON the rich development of aesthetic, scientific, and mathematical distancing arose other modes of understanding man, which were called forth initially by the practical exigencies of political life. The widespread success of Olympian religion, in leading the Greeks into axial existence, made possible a new form of government in which the masses of free citizens participated in basic political decisions. The road to power and influence in this context depended on the ability to persuade. Hence, there appeared teachers, whom we call Sophists, who were prepared to instruct ambitious young men in the arts of rhetoric.

To be able to persuade others, one must be well informed oneself and be able to reason clearly. At the same time, although democracy presupposed a basic rationality on the part of the citizens, few Greeks were under the illusion that men acted according to principles of reason alone. To learn to persuade others effectively, one must understand the nonrational factors in man alongside the rational and also understand how these interact. Hence, the nature of man himself had to be directly considered. Furthermore, some attention had to be given to the ends for which the power involved in the mastery of rhetoric was to be used.

These questions of the nature of man and the goal of life remained peripheral to the concerns of the Sophists as a class. Nevertheless, their presence created a new reflective awareness of aspects of human existence hitherto little recognized. Especially the questions of right and wrong arose in a rational sense quite alien to the Homeric tradition. This situation provided for the possibility of the appearance of

Socrates. With him, the two questions of the purpose of life and the nature of man moved to the center of the stage. He was convinced that far more important than the knowledge of how to persuade men is the knowledge of the good to which they should be persuaded.

It is my thesis that, in conjunction with his profound reflections on the good and the thought about the nature of man bound up with it, Socrates entered into a new structure of existence.[18] Under his influence this structure of existence permeated important segments of Greek society.

Socrates shared with the more responsible Sophists the view that the good is to be correlated with the reflectively desired. But this could be interpreted in two directions according to the manner in which the process of distancing proceeded. The Sophists took for granted a demythologized world in which human behavior in its social context could be dispassionately studied. Man's wants and needs, intelligently appraised in terms of the total situation, constituted the basis on which judgments of ends were to be made. Man is the measure.

To Socrates, on the contrary, this view seemed entirely unsatisfactory. In his thought, the relation of the good and reflective desire was reversed. A man did not call things " good " because he desired them, rather, he desired them because he supposed them to be good. Here, the psychic act of distancing was applied to that quality of experience which gives rise to man's sense of the normative, and this was conceived as standing over against man, possessing just the objectivity that belongs to a visual form when it is distanced in aesthetic experience. Indeed, the visual imagery always clung to the forms or ideas.

However, at this point Socrates far transcended what the visual imagery would suggest. The form of the good was apprehended by reason and not by sight, and the good that was thus apprehended did not qualify the appearance of one man to another, but rather the soul of each man in itself. The good was a form that characterized the experient and rational subject himself rather than the observable appearance and behavior of others.

Socrates thus contrasted the reality of the experient and rational

[18] Some features of this new structure may be due to Orphic influence, but too little is reliably known of Orphicism to allow anything more than conjectures with respect to its influence on Socrates.

subject, the soul, with the world of appearance in a way quite new for Greek ethical thought. His aim, just as that of Homeric religion, was for human excellence, but whereas for Homeric religion this meant of public excellence of manner and action, for Socrates this meant the perfection of the soul as such. Beauty was a quality of soul rather than of visual form.

Socrates further concluded that it was better to suffer than to inflict injustice, for one might suffer injustice without loss of the intrinsic excellence of the soul, whereas the infliction of injustice was precisely the destruction of the soul's inherent goodness.

Our deeper interest, however, is not with the conceptual doctrine of Socrates, but with the structure of existence therein expressed. I have defined axial existence in terms of the movement of the seat of the soul to its reflective consciousness and its dominance over the unconscious. The movement was witnessed from an early point in the rise of Homeric religion as the mythical meanings became subject to rational and aesthetic organization rather than simply providing the context of meaning in which life is lived. But the emergence of the reflective consciousness as the seat of human existence did not necessarily entail an awareness by the soul of itself. In Greece, this emerged gradually and fleetingly with only vague recognition of the problems of the relations of the soul to the total psychophysical organism. In the discussion of Homeric man, we saw how men understood themselves not as subjects, or souls, but from the public world and in terms of their role and appearance in that world, or else identified themselves with the impersonal principle of reason.

First in Socrates did the individual soul attain to self-awareness in the sense of knowing itself as an object of its own inquiry and its own activity. Socrates knew himself to *be* his soul, hence to be an invisible reality quite other than the appearances of his body to other men. In this respect, he resembled the Hindu sages, who had come much earlier than the Greeks to a clear awareness of the soul in sharp antithesis to sensory appearances. Yet there was a profound and fateful difference between Socrates and the Hindu thinker. The latter saw the rational ego-consciousness in its anxiety and suffering as something to be escaped. He identified himself as an undifferentiated subject underlying and transcending the concrete particularity of the individualized soul. Socrates, in contrast, identified himself with the soul as such, or more precisely, with the active reason that was, for him, the true essence of the soul. Hence, whereas the Indian sage sought to disengage his true self from the reality or illusion of the particularized soul, Socrates sought to achieve the proper excellence of the soul. Hence in him, the reflective consciousness made the soul the object of its reflection to discover the soul's peculiar character and to achieve the ideal embodiment of that character.

In the preceding paragraph, the word " reason " has begun to play an important role. Prior to the preceding chapter, this word has been avoided, and reference has been made instead to rational consciousness. By rational consciousness is meant reflective consciousness insofar as the symbolization by which it is ordered conforms to the world as given in unreflective consciousness rather than in the autonomous activity of the unconscious. Such conformation is witnessed just as clearly by accurate descriptions of natural and historical events as by abstraction, generalization, and inference. It is rational consciousness, in this broad sense, that is characteristic of all axial men.

As rational consciousness grew in strength, it provided for the possibility also of such activities as abstraction, generalization, and inference. These activities and the capacity to carry them out constitute " reason." Since rational consciousness was highly developed in the preaxial civilizations, reason played in them an important role. In India, reason gained still further provinces of activity. Nevertheless, it was among the scientist-philosophers of Greece that reason was carried to the highest pitch of development and that the activity of reason came to be prized most highly for its own sake. It was in Greece that reason came to be most closely identified with man's essential nature. Socrates' identification of himself with his reason was one of the fateful events of history.

It may still not be clear in what way the self-identification with reason led to and expressed a new structure of existence rather than simply to a new idea about existence. Perhaps the novelty of the structure is more readily understood in contrast with Homeric man who lacked self-awareness of himself as subject. But the structure of existence that emerged in Socrates is also to be sharply differentiated from that of the highly self-aware Hindu. This is because with each different fundamental mode of self-identification, conscious or unconscious, there is associated a different structuring of the elements of the soul. When the Hindu identified himself with an undifferentiated reality beyond the experientially diversified soul, the various elements in the soul — its passions, appetites, hopes, fears, sense experience, and reason — were all indifferently there to be recognized, described, and ultimately experienced as so many mere psychic elements over against the true self. When Socrates, in contrast, identified himself with his reason, no transcendent self came into play. Instead, a deep divide was introduced within the soul itself between reason and all other elements of the soul. The soul experienced itself in terms of this duality, within which one part was self, the other, alien. Again, this was not a mere opinion about the soul, but a structuring of the elements within the soul determining the roles they could play in the ongoing psychic life.

Given this structuring of the soul's life, a man's proper excellence must be the perfect dominance of his reason over all other elements of his psychic and physical life. The astounding greatness of Socrates was that he not only pioneered a new structure of psychic existence, but that, at the same time, he embodied this existence in ideal form. His own life and death were in perfect harmony with his teaching. In him, reason did triumph over the forces of the unconscious and the body and attain just that excellence it sought. He made no effort to attain pleasure or success, on the one hand, or the admiration of his fellows, on the other. He sought continuously to bring others to the knowledge of the truth regardless of what injustice this might cause *them* to inflict on *him*. Even when on trial for his life, he attempted to use the occasion to bring the Athenians to the truth rather than employing the rhetorical devices by which he could play on their sympathy. Thus he went to a voluntary death as the completion and fulfillment of a life dedicated to the good. In terms of the structure of existence he embodied, Socrates is not only unsurpassed but unsurpassable.

It has been emphasized that the psychic act of distancing underlay the peculiar structures of Greek existence in the axial period. This idea had quite ready application to Homeric man for whom man was understood as he was given in visual experience. However, its relevance to Socrates is far less obvious, for Socrates knew man as a rational subject.

Nevertheless, Socrates' understanding of man can also be seen as presupposing and involving a new level of the basic psychic act of distancing. This further level of distancing is similar in some respects to that involved in Greek mathematics where, on the one hand, one had to abstract from the visual forms in order to distance the quantitative forms, but, on the other hand, the quantitative forms remained tinged by the kind of spatiality known in vision. For Socrates, the soul was certainly *not* an object in the visual field (nor a quantitative form), yet insofar as it was conceptually grasped, the imagery carried a visual flavor. More important, this meant that for Socrates the categories in which he thought about the soul were derived from the experience of the world as it was given especially in vision. This meant also that in the process of thinking about the soul, the soul was distanced as object. The soul that was thought about was not the soul that was thinking in its dynamic immediacy, but an objectified, and thereby distanced, entity.

While emphasizing the amazing achievement of Socrates, we should not overlook the limitations inherent in Socratic existence. These limitations were inevitable, given the primacy of the psychic act of distancing as the foundation of Greek existence. The soul seen in this way, and therefore also the soul that came into existence in this way, could only be understood as made up of a plurality of elements or forces such as appetite, spirit, and reason. The interaction of such forces must be a function of their essentially impersonal activities. What the total soul was or became was the resultant of these forces. There could be no freedom or transcendence by the self over these forces.

In this context, a self that was identified with reason always, by definition, behaved rationally. If the soul as a whole did not behave rationally, this could only mean that the other, and hence alien, forces in the soul had been stronger. The rational self could hardly be responsible for its defeat by these irrational forces.

Socrates certainly is not to be understood as simply and fully acquiescing in the implications of his conceptual situation. He accepted responsibility for the victory of reason within his own soul in a way that implied an inner transcendence over the irrational and rational forces alike. Furthermore, he exhorted others to live by reason in a way that assumed a transcendent responsibility also on their part. Nevertheless, the limitation remained. The transcendent selfhood was unrecognized and, therefore, was only incipiently effective. In their brilliant ethical reflections, the Greeks always explained failure to do the good in such a way that from our point of view no real responsibility therefor can be attributed to the wrongdoer. The clear emergence of responsible personhood, with the quite different categories and problems it entailed, occurred only in Israel and will be the subject of the next chapter.

That the Greeks interpreted man in terms of categories derived from the distancing of the world, and that this entailed certain limitations in the apprehension of personal responsibility, should not be difficult to understand in our day. Modern psychology has been basically Greek, and its two major forms, academic psychology and depth psychology, have remarkable analogies respectively with Homeric and Socratic views of man.

In modern academic psychology, one attempts to gain knowledge of man through careful observation of his behavior in controlled situations. This observation is primarily visual, although the visual data can be supplemented by other sensory information. The man observed is asked questions, and his answers are recorded. But when the psychologist is most " scientific," he regards these answers as a part of the behavior of the subject and not as a source of knowledge of some inner, unobservable state. The theories about man that are scientifically developed avoid positing any such inner state. This means that very intensive efforts are made to understand man according to forms and methods applicable in man's knowledge of the rest of the natural world.

Depth psychology, of course, is very different. Here the reports of the patient or subject about his inner life are taken very seriously. A whole world of reality is assumed that is not directly observable by the scientist. Observable behavior is interpreted as to its meaning according to the categories of understanding developed in relation to this inner world. Nevertheless, also in most depth psychology, the categories by which the inner world is understood are modeled on the forms observed through the senses in the outer world. The id, the ego, and the superego, for example, are treated as entities or forces whose interactions are not unlike those of entities or forces observed by physics or chemistry. Psychic states and overt behavior are interpreted as the outcome of the interaction of these several forces.

Since these forces are themselves fundamentally impersonal, their resultant in feeling and action cannot be a person in the sense in which Hebrew man came to understand himself. The " I " or " ego " is one force alongside others, to be understood in its functioning according to psychic laws having the same deterministic character as natural laws. In actual practice, the psychoanalyst does attribute to the " I " of his patient a greater transcendence over these psychic forces than his theories justify, just as the academic psychologist, consciously or unconsciously, attributes to his subjects an inwardness that his science ignores. The point is that, even today when we attempt to develop a conceptual scheme for the understanding of man, we ordinarily bring to our task an understanding of concepts and a set of concepts which arise in our dealings with the external world as mediated by sense experience. It is certainly not surprising that the Greeks, who first discovered and achieved the possibility of observing the external world as such, should have proceeded in the same manner.

There is, however, also a difference between the situation of the Greeks in this respect and modern man. Modern man somehow knows that the scientific picture of himself is an abstraction. This is more glaringly true of the picture drawn by academic psychology than of that drawn by depth psychology. But even with respect to the latter, wide segments of the intellectual community know that the individual man cannot finally be grasped in the impersonal categories that constitute the science. Alongside the scientific understanding of man in impersonal categories, there are passionately personalistic protests that play a very large role in our art and culture.

We should not expect to find this among the Greeks. Western man has entered into a personalistic individualism out of centuries of interaction with the Biblical God. Hence, this individuality and personality cannot simply disappear when his conceptual theories cease to justify them and his religious practices cease to reinforce them. There remains a powerful tension between what man knows himself to be in his immediate givenness to himself and what he is taught conceptually about himself. This tension is at the heart of the peculiarly modern experience of anxiety and meaninglessness in which a person, who is formed in a context of meaning, finds himself attempting to understand himself in categories that preclude the possibility of meaning. But this was not the situation of Greek man. He did not know himself as a person in the modern sense. There was little tension at this point between his art and his science. His conceptual self-understanding in terms of reason and passion corresponded to his existence as it was given to him. The question of the relation of himself as person to these impersonal forces which constituted him hardly arose, except insofar as he might identify one or the other of these forces as alien to his true humanity.

The achievement of Socrates was, then, that in him the seat of individual existence became firmly identified with reason. Further, reason knew itself as such and was able to understand and deal with other aspects of the psychic life from this new perspective. The limitation which has been noted was that Socratic man's self-identification with one factor within the soul alongside other factors prevented the incipient sense of personal responsibility for the psychic life in general from coming to fruition.

In the discussion of Socratic existence, only Socrates himself has been treated. In conclusion, it should be made clear that the kind of existence ideally embodied in him is reflected also in most of the Greek and Roman philosophy that followed him and looked back to him with special reverence. We can assume that what was expressed in this literature was also widely prevalent among cultivated people other than writers, and that it has continued to our own day as a viable and influential structure of existence.

What is common to all these embodiments of Socratic existence is that the self is identified with reason. Other factors in the life of the soul and body are objectified from this point of view as other and alien. But this fundamental common starting point allows for great diversity of development according to how reason is understood. There is a great difference, for example, between the Stoics, on the one hand, and Aristotle, on the other. However, for the purposes of this book, their unity is of paramount interest.

Chapter Nine

PROPHETIC EXISTENCE

IN THEIR AXIAL DEVELOPMENT, the Indians turned their attention on the problem of salvation. They accepted the ancient understanding of a meaningless and endless succession of states and experience and undertook to find the way in which this could be brought to an end. The Greeks, by contrast, employed their growing powers of reason to order the world about them and then to discover the order objectively present in that world. They turned only later to the investigation of the soul and the quest for salvation, and when they did so, they employed the types of categories they had used so successfully in their understanding of the outer world.

The Hebrews adopted a third path. As their power of rational reflection grew, they accepted the tribal myth of a divine lawgiver, much as the Indians accepted the myth of transmigration and the Greeks that of their ancestral gods. Their critical and reflective activity was directed toward rationalizing the understanding of their relationship to this deity. This unconscious decision turned out to be just as determinative of their whole cultural and intellectual development as had the corresponding choices in India and Greece for those civilizations.

Old Testament scholarship is currently in a state of flux, such that any attempt to state just where and how axial existence emerged in Israel must be very tentative. Our future understanding depends on the outcome of new research on the relation of wisdom tradition to the cult and of both to the prophets. In any case, the shift of the seat of existence to reflective consciousness is witnessed to in writings dating back to the time of David, if not earlier.

Our interest, however, is not in the scattered and partial foreshadowings of the axial revolution, but in its decisive and distinctive embodiment. In India, this embodiment was to be found in the rise of the philosophical schools of the sixth century B.C. This presupposed an extensive preparation in the preceding centuries, a preparation already witnessed to in the Upanishads. But this preparation alone would not have transformed India into an axial culture, any more than parallel developments in the rationalization of culture and religion qualified Egypt as the seat of an axial revolution.

When the question is raised with respect to Israel in these terms, the claim of the prophetic movement of the eighth and seventh centuries to be the bearer of the axial revolution stands vindicated. Hence, this chapter is entitled, "Prophetic Existence." I see in the great prophets — and especially in Jeremiah — the decisive breakthrough into a new structure of existence.

Just as "Homeric existence" has been used to mean not only or primarily the existence reflected and expressed in the Homeric epics but, rather, the existence that came into being among those whose vision was formed by this literature, so here "prophetic existence" does not refer to that which was distinctive of the prophets alone, but, rather, to that which became distinctive of Israel as a result of their impact. This impact was mediated as much through the Deuteronomic code as through the remembered and written words of the prophets themselves.

The idea of a divine lawgiver was a commonplace among ancient peoples, and it played some role in almost all religions. However, for Socratic man this idea was not determinative for the axial development. Insofar as the Olympian gods were dissociated from fate, their role as ground and authority of law declined. As the Greeks progressed in their application of reason to the understanding of law, they developed quite naturalistic ideas of how law arose in social community. If deity played any role, it was as reason, the immanent principle in man and the world. Insofar as the idea of the divine lawgiver remained among the Greeks, it was as a part of the lingering power of myth.

With the Hebrews, the situation was quite different. To them it was clear that they existed as a community by virtue of their relation to deity, and, indeed, to a specific deity, Yahweh. The essential task of reflection was to understand this relation, and that meant to understand the participants in this relation. Especially, this meant that man must understand the divine side of this relation.

To understand Yahweh was, of course, not to objectify and localize him as an entity to be observed. It was, rather, to understand what he was in his relation to Israel. How was the relation established? What was expected of Israel? What benefits accrued from maintaining the relation? How could specific events be understood in the light of this relation?

The relation of Yahweh and Israel was understood commonly in terms of the category of covenant. Again, this understanding as such, although far from universal among ancient peoples, was not peculiar to Israel. Other peoples also thought of their relation to their gods in terms of mutual obligations. They too expected that if they fulfilled their responsibilities to the god, the god should and would fulfill his responsibilities to them. They also understood plague and defeat in terms of failure on their part to fulfill their obligations to the god.

The Hebrew understanding of the covenant with God showed its distinctiveness much more clearly at the point of the divine initiative. I do not know to what extent other views of covenant relations of peoples with gods included this element of the divine initiative. But it is safe to say that with no other people did this become the foundation of the self-understanding of the community as it did in Israel. Israel understood itself as chosen by Yahweh for this covenant relation prior to any act or understanding on its own part. The covenant followed the election, its terms were set entirely by God, the people were confronted by one great choice — to accept or to reject the covenant freely offered by the God who had already chosen them without respect to their worthiness.

The kind of reflection that was involved in articulating this understanding of Israel's relation to its God was at much the same level of sophistication as that displayed by Homer in his poetic objectification, aestheticizing, and ordering of the gods. It had, however, an entirely different consequence. Whereas the Greek poets and artists freed the Greek mind to enjoy the forms of the world as they were, the original Hebrew achievement determined that Yahweh, in his relation to Israel, must be the focus of concern of the whole people. Since this relation was an intelligible one of choice and offer on Yahweh's part and agreement on the part of the people, it allowed for and encouraged further rationalization. But the kind of rationalization appropriate to the understanding of Yahweh's choice of Israel and Israel's proper response was very different from that of the Greeks.

The Hebrew understanding of Yahweh was thoroughly anthropomorphic, just as was the Homeric understanding of the Greek gods. Yet, the anthropomorphism involved was of a radically different kind. Greek anthropomorphism was fundamentally the picturing of the gods as ideal humans, and this, at the Homeric stage of development, meant humans who were beautiful, wise, and powerful. They existed as objects of imaginative visual contemplation. They engaged in more or less serious play with each other and with the destinies of men and cities.

Yahweh was completely unlike the Olympian pantheon. Even in those few remaining references from an early stage of the development in which he was pictured almost as a man among men, there was no suggestion as to his appearance. Yahweh's relationship to man was almost entirely verbal. He commanded and promised, and, of course, he fulfilled his promises both for good and ill. He did not present himself to man for aesthetic contemplation but for dialogue and obedience. To put it quite simply, Yahweh was not seen, but heard.

This did not mean, in the first instance, some more sophisticated view of God — as invisible and intangible. Perhaps it even meant a less sophisticated view in the sense that reason did not dare to deal with the sacred power. God did not appear visually, not because he, in principle, was invisible, but because one could not see God and live. The Hebrews never domesticated Yahweh as the Greeks domesticated their pantheon.

However, the important question is not that of comparative sophistication but of further consequences for development. Yahweh was anthropomorphic in the sense that man attributed to him some of the emotions he found in himself — hate and love, anger and repentance. But Yahweh was far too sacred for Hebrew man to think of him at play or as engaged in frivolous pursuits. Also, Yahweh was not surrounded by a pantheon of other deities. His social relations were with the world and, specifically, with Israel.

I have spoken of the Hebrew view of Yahweh as anthropomorphic. In a sense this is true, but insofar as it implies the application to Yahweh of a preexisting understanding of man, it is misleading. Hebrew reflection about Yahweh led to an understanding of Yahweh as person long before men could conceive themselves in such terms. Certainly Yahweh is understood in the light of Hebrew man's vague understanding of himself. But the clarification and development of human self-understanding was for Hebrew man a function of his beliefs about Yahweh. It is important to make this point because of the widespread assumption that man's self-understanding develops autonomously and is projected on other things. But neither with the Greeks nor with the Hebrews is this a useful way of understanding the actual course of the development. In both cases, reflection developed its categories in its attempt to understand something other than man. In both cases, this activity had profound consequences for man's self-understanding.

Although the explicit denial of bodily form to Yahweh was late, the early depreciation of interest in any such question forced Hebrews to think of God in some other way. This was a matter of utmost importance. To this day, and despite the immense impact of the Hebraic achievement on our psychic life, our imagery and conceptualization is primarily visual. When I think of a friend, some visual image presents itself to me, and although my thought of him may have many other facets, I tend to think that these other facets are to be referred to this visual one. Many people find that belief in God is impossible for them precisely because they can form no visual image of him.

Thus the Hebrews confronted an immensely difficult psychic task. Their rational attention centered on Yahweh, yet they had to think of Yahweh fundamentally without visual images. In India, also, it is true, the holy power was finally conceived as transcending all sensory forms, but there it was recognized that the contemplation of Brahman in this ultimate way could only be the fruit of intense psychic discipline accompanied by highly abstruse metaphysical reflection. Neither this psychic discipline nor the metaphysical reflection was available to the Hebrew mind. It was in this situation that a vague mode of understanding emerged among the Hebrews, which can best be pointed to in our vocabulary by the idea of person. God was understood as the great " I," who spoke and acted, thought and decided.

Once we understand the Hebrew success in conceiving Yahweh as the great " I," we can see that Hebrew reflection, or perhaps better, Hebrew experience with Yahweh, led to the explicit rejection of the idea that he had bodily form or was localized in spatial terms. The great " I," who was bound by no form and hence by no place, was progressively understood to be fully independent of his people and their cultic worship. He dwelt in no man-made building, and he was incomparably superior to those deities which did. Indeed, those deities were not really gods at all, but merely objects made by human hands and absurdly worshiped. Yahweh alone was God.

Furthermore, this understanding of the great " I," who was alone God, made possible a new understanding of the relation of God and the world. When the gods were understood either mythically or in visual images, they could be understood as powerful forces in the production of the universe, but not in a radical sense as creators. They were too much a part of the world to call it into being. In any case, to the rational mind the attribution of the world to the activities of other visually conceivable entities could, at best, only push the question of origins back one step. Much more acceptable to reason was the other conception of the world as eternal and of the gods as ultimately part of that eternal world.

The Hebrew understanding of the great " I " allowed an alternative view. The decay that beset all visible things did not apply to him. He dwelt forever, independent of the existence of any other reality, and if a world existed at all, it was because he willed it. Perhaps some primal chaos also existed from all eternity. If so, God is still not to be viewed as participating in it or as dependent on it. But whether out of nothing or out of primal chaos, God called the world into being.

Since God was not anthropomorphic in the sense of having physical form, but only in the sense of being a subject who spoke and acted, the Biblical story of creation did not picture one who molded primeval matter into new shapes, but one who spoke and thereby effected his will. Here was a vision of creation that made clear the relation of radical dependence of the world on God and elevated the relation of creator-creature into the fundamental context for all understanding of man himself.

Israel understood itself first in the context of the covenant. It existed as a corporate body elected by God and confronted by him with a demand and a promise. In relation to that confrontation, it could make a choice of acceptance or rejection, obedience or disobedience. This choice was not necessitated by outward forces or inner psychic mechanisms. It was made in the encounter relation with God. Israel was fully responsible for its choice and must rightfully suffer the consequence when it disobeyed.

We have here, from an early time, the development of fundamentally ethical categories for understanding the human situation in a way quite different from Indians and Greeks. Of course, taboos played a large role in all three cultures, but in the axial period they were understood differently by each culture. In India, the movement into the inner depths of the individual psyche radically relativized the question of the taboo, leaving the taboo system largely effective in society at large but making it quite irrelevant to the enlightened man. In Greece, the taboos were there, and their force was acknowledged, but it was the path of courage, the task of the hero, to flout them. Among the Hebrews, the whole content of the taboo system was identified with the demand of God embodied in the covenant. Hence, obedience to the individual demands, however meaningless they might be in themselves, took on the character of moral virtue, because it meant obedience to the will of God. The goal of the community was to achieve righteousness, which meant conformity to the will of God.

Although from one point of view this exaltation of the taboos into the will of the personal deity was an impediment to rationality, in another respect it created the context in which rationality could enter into genuinely ethical reflection. Where the taboos were simply pushed aside by reason, as in India and Greece, rational reflection on the nature of the good life became possible, but the sense of ought, expressed so powerfully in the taboos, remained unrationalized, whereas among the Hebrews the question of what one ought to do preoccupied rational attention. Hence, despite frequent setbacks, the Hebrews began to rationalize the sense of obligation.

The process of rationalization reflected in the great prophets was not one of deliberate reflection. Rather, the apprehension of the supreme " I " was such that certain cultic practices and taboos associated with his worship appeared altogether irrelevant. They had grown up out of archaic religion and continued in little broken continuity with it. God, as now apprehended by axial man, was seen as radically opposed to all that. He was seen as opposed to every practice or idea that implied some sacredness of its own or of some special time and place. God's concern was with the communal life as such and not with any compartmentalized segment thereof. In particular, the prophets denounced the view that God could be kept satisfied by particular ceremonial acts, while the community as a whole forsook the patterns of life which the prophets associated with justice and righteousness.

The very intensity of the apprehension of God by the prophets led them to see this world as freed from the sacred meanings of the unconscious. Therefore, they could see God's will, and hence man's responsibilities in this world, not in terms of the inherited taboo system, but in terms of what their new apprehension of God in itself indicated. This made possible rational alteration and interpretation of the taboos leading to the possibility of critical reflection about them.

This process was analogous to what occurred in Greece, but also very different. Among the Greeks, the world was objectified in such a way that the forms of rational reflection came to be determined by the forms given in the world instead of by the unconscious and its projections. Among the Hebrews, God and his will were recognized as other in such a way that it became possible to understand what man ought to do in terms of the new understanding of God instead of in terms of the taboos that belong to the unconscious life. In principle, the great eighth-century prophets already achieved this radical breakthrough, but we know that, as assimilated into the religious tradition of Israel, their impact was to modify and supplement the structure of law that still retained much from its archaic sources.

In the eighth-century prophets, the vision was still one in which Yahweh and the nation were the covenant partners. It was the people as a whole who had sinned against God and who must suffer the just consequences of their disobedience. But by the seventh century, the collective personality of the people was giving way to the individual. According to Amos, the justice of God would bring destruction on the nation. But Jeremiah wondered why God allowed individual wicked men to prosper while individual righteous men suffered. He could not accept the view that the children should suffer for the sins of their parents and grandparents. This shift from the understanding of the people as a whole as the covenant partner of God to the idea that God deals with individuals as individuals is of such importance that we must pause to consider how it may have developed.

I have suggested that the eighth-century prophets presented the dealings of God as being with his people as a whole. Nevertheless, the sins that they denounced were not only acts of which the corporate body, represented in its rulers, was guilty. They were also sins of individual members of society, the sins of the rich and powerful against the poor and weak. The earlier prophets may have thought of these individual sins as the sins of the community as a whole; nevertheless, in a civilized posttribal community, they could not be seen *only* in that light. It would be natural to make distinctions between, for example, some men who responded to the prophets' message by taking such action as they could, such as the disciples of Isaiah, and those others who were indifferent and self-satisfied. The distinction of the obedient and the disobedient would run through the community.

Since God was now thought of quite personally, it would be natural to think of him also as recognizing the distinction between the obedient and the disobedient members of the community and, hence, of differentiating his dealings between these. Insofar as this was the case, it became a matter of the individual's decision as to how to align his life. The decision for obedience or disobedience, which, as late as the eighth century, remained primarily communal, now became primarily individual. This meant that a man could no longer understand himself exclusively as a part of the community. Rather, he must begin to understand the community as composed of individuals.

Another factor of equal importance must be considered in this period. Down through the eighth century, although God was understood as Person, individual men were still thought of chiefly as they appeared to one another. This did not lead to seeing men in aesthetic categories as with the Greeks, but it did focus attention on overt behavior. Decision or choice was not understood as some inner psychic struggle but as the action itself. The laws that embodied God's will, whether primitive taboos or the demand of justice and mercy, regulated overt acts. As long as the agent of activity was primarily the corporate body, nothing else was possible.

But as the individual found himself the agent of decision, new factors entered in. Placed in decision by the confrontation with God as mediated by the prophetic word, the individual was aware that decision was not simply an action, that it might involve a struggle prior to overt action, and that sometimes the conscious decision did not carry over into the action pursued. Men became aware of their " heart " as not simply the seat of emotions and feelings but as involved in willing or choosing as well.

Furthermore, since God was not thought of as himself a visible reality but, rather, as an invisible " I," God might be thought of as taking an interest in this inner struggle for and against obedience to his will. Indeed, God might be supposed to be related to man fundamentally at that point where he was most like him, that is, in his mind, soul, or heart, rather than in his observable behavior. Perhaps God judged men finally more by this inner invisible reality than by the overt actions in terms of which men judge each other.

We should not suppose that such extreme conclusions were ever widely and clearly drawn among the Hebrews. Their sense of corporate existence remained extremely strong, and their focus of attention, as far as man is concerned, remained on that which is overt and visible, that which has public consequences. Nevertheless, the concern for the heart, the inner man, existed and persisted as a subdominant theme of Hebrew life.

The combination of the understanding of the individual as the one addressed by God, and thereby placed in decision, and the awareness of the inwardness of the decision joined in producing that peculiar kind of responsible, self-conscious individuality which justifies the term " person." The person, in this sense of the term, emerged clearly for the first time in seventh-century Israel. Jeremiah is the striking example.

This new structure of existence is peculiarly difficult to describe for two reasons. First, whereas both the Indians and the later Greeks were able to analyze the structures of their own existence with remarkable detachment and philosophical skill, no comparable self-objectification or philosophical ability is to be found among the Hebrews of the axial period. Second, to this day, the meaning of " I " remains peculiarly elusive among those whose existence is formed through Israel's history. Yet something must be said.

Obviously, the use of the first person singular pronoun or some grammatical equivalent is universal. Some way of distinguishing the speaker from other men is possible and normal in any language. The question is, What is thereby referred to? One possibility is that the referent be one organism among others, namely, the one that is speaking, and this possibility is actualized frequently, even among us. It may even be regarded as the " natural " understanding of " I," and this for the following reason.

Man's conscious experience has as its ordinary object not itself but the world, and especially the sensuously given world. In this world, man distinguishes individuals on some of whom his comfort and well-being depend. Gradually, he becomes aware that these important individuals, in their turn, perceive him in the same way in which he perceives them. By seeing his reflection, he gains an impression of what he is in their eyes. He thus becomes conscious of himself as one among the many individuals presented to each other through sense experience. To differentiate this individual from others, he speaks of " I."

In Socratic man, we noted a further development of great importance. Man became aware of processes of desiring, feeling, and reasoning as something other than the sensuously observable. These forces were seen as separately individualized in a special relation to each human body. Hence, the first person singular could refer to the invisible soul in distinction to the visible body. Within the soul, further distinctions were made, for example, between reason and desire, and the seat of existence was identified with reason. This was not simply an intellectual theory about the structures of existence, but a new structuring of existence in which the nonrational forces in the soul were objectified from the perspective of reason. Of course, much of the functioning of the soul is unaltered by the presence or absence of theories about it, but in humanly crucial respects, the elements attaining consciousness and the roles which they play in consciousness are profoundly interrelated in axial man with the way in which he understands himself.

In characterizing Socratic man, use of the term "person" was avoided. This is because the soul, although clearly individual, was understood primarily as the product of nonpersonal forces. That is, passion and reason, though numerically individuated in each soul, were forces for whose characterization the individuality of the particular soul was unimportant. The souls were qualitatively differentiated only according to the relative power of the several forces within them.

The greatest of the Greeks, such as Socrates, did approximate to personal existence. That is, Socrates did in fact assume responsibility for the victory of his reason over his passions, a responsibility that is not intelligible if we think of his soul as only a composite of these forces. But in his own conceptuality, no place for such transcendence was possible, and he himself came to the conclusion that to know the good was to do it.

Where conscious thought and available conceptuality run counter to the idea of responsibility for one's use of reason and obedience to it, even if the transcendence involved in such responsibility remains incipiently present, it cannot emerge as the organizing principle of the soul. Hence, full personhood could not develop within Greek culture.

These negative statements may serve to illumine what positively the personal structure of existence was. It presupposed, of course, the emergence of rational consciousness and the location of the seat of existence within it that was characteristic of all axial men. It presupposed within the complexity of the conscious life of the soul a multiplicity of conflicting forces. But the seat of existence from which these forces were viewed, and in some measure objectified, could not be identified with any of them. It was, rather, a center that had no given character of its own other than that of being in each new situation concretely responsible for the soul's total response. This transcendent, responsible center is the " personal I," and with its emergence every other element within the soul comes to play a different role.[19]

[19] It is tempting to call the new emergent the will, and this is plausible and even helpful. The difficulty is only that the term " will " suggests one factor in the soul alongside others. Reason and passion were in this way recognized as competing forces by the Greeks. But for the Hebrews, what emerged was not one more such factor but a new center, given as the " I," from which all choosing must be carried out. Only when this, in turn, was relativized from the perspective of spiritual existence can we speak appropriately of will.

Chapter Ten

CHRISTIAN EXISTENCE

IN ALL AXIAL MEN, the seat of existence is located in the rational consciousness. But in India from this organizing center the thinker had sought a " self " beyond it. In so doing, he had attempted to overcome that structure of existence given to him as an axial man. Gautama had rejected this quest for a transcendent self, and he purified the reflective consciousness from the last traces of mythical influence. This, he believed, also broke the power of the bond that held the successive moments of experience together in the unity we have called the soul. In the process, therefore, reason was vigorously active, but the goal of this activity was a final passivity of the reflective consciousness toward what is given in the unreflective consciousness. Homeric man distanced the world aesthetically and projected into that distance both the numinous powers and his own motives and emotions. Insofar as he was conscious of himself, it was of himself as he appeared in the public world. Socrates identified himself with his reason, now understood as active conscious thought based on what is given by the unreflective consciousness and tested against it. The resultant bifurcation of the soul passed through the reflective consciousness itself, recognizing the emotions as part of that consciousness but regarding them as alien to the self. Prophetic man accepted responsibility for the outcome of the conflict of forces within his soul, thereby identifying himself with a center transcending reason and passion alike.

It is now time to turn directly to that subject which is the controlling interest of the entire book. What is Christianity, and specifically, what is the structure of Christian existence in relation to all these other structures of existence?

Christian existence arose out of prophetic existence in much the same way that Socratic existence arose out of Homeric existence.[20] Socratic existence could not have arisen apart from the prior distancing of the world and the discovery of the forms it embodies. Similarly, Christian existence could not have arisen apart from that responsibility for one's acts before God that constituted personal existence. But despite this parallelism, there were great differences in the course of development in Greece and Palestine.

In postexilic Judaism, prophetic existence was widely and firmly established. By the time of Jesus, the Jewish people as a whole were formed by this type of axial existence. This does not mean, however, that they continued, unaltered, the experience or the beliefs of the prophets. In this book, " Homeric existence " has meant that structure of existence which was nurtured in Greece under the influence of the Homeric writings. Similarly, " prophetic existence " means that structure of existence which arose in Israel as a result of the prophetic movement. Israel appropriated the prophetic message and entered into prophetic existence without abandoning its cultic traditions or overcoming the archaic elements in its law.

The institution through which prophetic existence was effectively transmitted from generation to generation was the synagogue. The rabbis who taught in the synagogues held varied opinions on many matters, but when we view them as a whole in their relation to non-Jewish developments and to heretical movements (such as Gnosticism), we are impressed by their unity. The clearest embodiment of that general orientation which dominated the synagogues is to be found in the Pharisees. The Gospels themselves selected Pharisaism as the representative form of Judaism in relation to which what was new in Jesus could be most clearly seen. Unfortunately, this use of Pharisaism in the Gospels has led to a pejorative connotation that is wholly unjustified. The role of Pharisaism in relation to Christianity is properly seen only when it is recognized that despite its marked divergence from the prophets, especially in its understanding of the law, it was, in Jesus' day, the finest flowering of

[20] See the Appendix for a discussion of the alternate view that Gnosticism is the parent of Christianity.

prophetic existence and the worthiest alternative to Christianity.

In this chapter, Pharisaism is chosen to represent the determinative form taken by prophetic existence in Jesus' day. Jesus' message is presented over against Pharisaic Judaism rather than directly in relation to the prophets themselves. In part, it should be understood as a renewal of the distinctively prophetic element within the Pharisaic synthesis. But this is true only in part, for the result transcended not only the particular form of prophetic existence embodied in Pharisaism, but also the prophets themselves.

This selection of Pharisaism expresses the belief not only that Pharisaism represented the normative expression of the mainstream of prophetic Judaism, but also that Jesus' message formed itself primarily in relation to Pharisaism out of a different configuration of elements in this mainstream. Much the same could be said of the Essene communities, who in some respects resembled and differed from the Pharisees in the same way as Jesus. In other respects, the Hellenization of Judaism in the diaspora led to developments parallel to Christianity. Indeed, the possibility of crossing a threshold like that crossed by Christianity has been a permanent characteristic of Judaism, even apart from Christian influence. If my interest were to demonstrate the uniqueness of the several elements in Jesus' message and Christian experience, it would be essential to make comparison with all forms of Judaism. However, my interest lies in the actual and effective emergence of a new structure of existence, and as a matter of historical fact, this occurred only by the total impact of Jesus' transformation of Jewish teaching combined with his resurrection appearances. The initial and decisive impact was made chiefly on those whose beliefs had previously been most fully articulated by the Pharisees.

In previous chapters, the structures of existence have been discussed with little attention to the relation between those through whom the new structures received their shape and those who later participated in them. This does not mean that there were no differences. Certainly, there were great differences between the creators of the Homeric epics and the Greek tragedians. Similarly, whereas Socrates cannot be understood apart from his daemon, this was not mentioned, because nothing comparable played a role in Socratic existence generally. The several expressions of prophetic existence differed from the prophetic message itself, and the structure of the existence of the prophets themselves included a relation to God in which prophetic existence generally did not participate. This difference was neglected in the previous chapter, but we must return to it below in attempting to understand Jesus' relation to his heritage.

When we come to the rise of Christian existence, we cannot continue to neglect the question of the difference in the structure of existence of those responsible for its emergence and of those who followed. Jesus and the Easter experiences of the community were the occasion for crossing the new threshold. But there were special features in Jesus' relation to God and in the experience of the Holy Spirit in the early church that, while essential to the original transition into Christian existence, are not typically present in that existence. The distinction here is fundamentally of the same order as the other distinctions mentioned, but it has played a much larger role in Christian self-understanding than have the parallel distinctions elsewhere.

In recognition of this situation, this chapter is divided into two main sections treating, respectively, the message of Jesus and the primitive Christian experience of the postresurrection church. This would allow also for discussion of the structures of existence of Jesus and of the primitive Christian, conscious of the indwelling presence of the divine Spirit, in their distinctiveness from that of later believers.

However, such discussions would carry us too far in the direction of Christology and pneumatology, subjects which require extensive treatment in their own right and would distract us here from our central concern. Hence, they are dealt with only to that degree which is necessary for the understanding of the rise of normal Christian existence; and in the explicit treatment of structures of existence at the end of the chapter, only that structure of existence in which Christians generally have shared is considered.

Pharisaism combined an intense ethical consciousness with a future hope. In this combination, it was essentially faithful to its prophetic heritage. Yet, both in its ethical consciousness and in its hope, it lacked one feature characteristic of the prophets themselves. The prophets had known God as present, living, acting reality, but for the Jews of the postexilic period, God was silent and remote. The acts of God were in the past or, hopefully, in the future. As long as God was experienced in his remoteness, nothing else was possible.

The central and decisive fact in the appearance of Jesus was the renewal of the sense of the present immediacy of God. Such a statement hardly does full justice to the remarkable character of this occurrence, since by the use of the term " renewal " it suggests something of a return to an earlier condition. If this were all that were involved, such a renewal might well have been a common occurrence in postexilic Judaism. I suggest that it was not a common occurrence precisely because of the success of the prophetic faith. Some explanation of this point is needed.

Mythical man lived in a universe of sacred meanings and powers. This sacred power was bound up with the unconscious and with its products in consciousness. The shift of the seat of existence from the unconscious to the conscious estranged the self from the sacred power, and the triumph of the rational conciousness over the mythical broke also the power of the sacred. Therefore, the freedom of axial man was also the possibility of freedom from deity. This freedom is to be found among both the Indians and the Greeks. In both cases, in freeing man from the power of myth, the axial development freed him also from the experience of living in relation to presently active divine powers, which took initiative in their dealings with men.

Among the Hebrews, however, the axial development retained the context of the divine-human relation. Here the mythical was ethicized and personalized. At the point of the transition toward this ethicizing and personalizing, the power of the sacred remained overwhelmingly present. But when by this act the sacred power was rationalized, it was also distanced. That is, when men had learned to understand God as a person and his will as a body of moral teaching, they continued to recognize his supreme importance for human life, but his actual present effectiveness became a matter of belief rather than of immediate apprehension.

Thus the centering of existence in consciousness, even in the Hebrew development, pushed the sacred power to the fringes of awareness. The belief that God acted became a part of the conscious, conceptual structure, but the action itself stood outside the sphere of conscious experience and was looked on as past and future rather than present. There seemed to be no way of recovering the vital immediacy of the relation to God, except by a return to the mythical existence of the preaxial state, a return to which Judaism was strictly opposed.

In terms of the nature of the axial transformation, the widespread estrangement from the divine is readily intelligible. Among the Indians and Greeks alike, there were attempts to transcend consciousness or to destroy it so as to recover a primeval condition of unity with the divine. Alternately, Aristotle pointed to the possibility of contemplation of a deity known through inference. But within the context of fully conscious existence, the divine as immediately experienced seemed to be almost necessarily pushed aside.

Yet in Jesus, the full responsible personhood of Hebrew axial man was combined, without loss, with an existence that found its content in the fully personal God. Jesus knew this God as he was taught to know him by the traditions of Israel. But Jesus' knowledge had an immediacy that transcended the authority of these traditions and enabled him to stand in judgment on them. He knew God as the presently active reality that had incomparably greater reality than the world of creaturely things. He lived and spoke out of the immediacy of this reality. Of course, the experiential immediacy of God to Jesus in no way meant that he was not also formed by the history and traditions of Israel.

Jesus' proclamation of the immediacy of God took the form of the proclamation of the imminence of his Kingdom, which meant the apocalyptic end. This was no accident. For him, no less than for the apocalyptic emphasis within Judaism, there was a total hiatus between what God was and the actual condition of his world. Hence, the nearness of God could only mean that this world could not stand before him.

Yet it is not enough to think of Jesus as an apocalyptic preacher, however true this may be, for his apocalypticism was quite distinct from that of mainstream Judaism. For the latter, the conviction of the apocalyptic end belonged with the experience of God's absence and remoteness. It was because one *believed* that God must vindicate the righteous that one knew that the transformation must come. But for Jesus, the apocalyptic message stemmed from the *awareness* of

God's nearness. Hence, the Kingdom was at hand, and, indeed, at hand in such a way as to be already effectively operative in the moment. The difficulty of unraveling the elements of futuristic and realized eschatology in the message of Jesus stems from the fact that, far more basic for him than any conceptual scheme of the sequence of events, was the fact of God's present reality to him and for him. That present reality meant that God was effectively active in that *now*. It meant also that the world as it was constituted in that now was already on the point of dissolution.

Just as Jesus accepted the apocalyptic elements in Judaism, so also he accepted other aspects of contemporary Jewish doctrine and ethical concern. But to these, too, he gave a formulation quite distinct from that of Pharisaism.

In principle, some of the prophetic utterances point to a total ethicizing of the understanding of God's will. But in fact this did not occur among the Jews. Rather, the taboo system was taken up into the understanding of the will of God. There it was, to some degree, ethicized in its particulars, but it remained incompletely rationalized. Obedience to any item of the law was in itself an ethical act, and in this sense, the relation of the individual to God was ethicized. Interpretation and application could do much to rationalize the arbitrary features of the legal code, but as long as this code was fixed as the past word of God, and as long as God was understood to have spoken in the past rather than in the present, complete rationalization could not occur. Thus the Pharisees, despite their highly developed ethical self-consciousness, and despite the fact that their rabbis were able to point to love of God and man as the sum of the law, remained bound to prerational requirements in the name of ethics. This bred among them also an elaborate casuistry as they attempted to derive intelligible and practical guidance from rules that reflected an archaic, mythical mentality.

Jesus' renewal of the prophetic consciousness of God in the context of fully responsible personhood broke through the limits of the old law. The distinction between ethical principles, on the one hand, and ancient taboos and cultic rules, on the other, may have been tentatively and provisionally made by some Pharisees, but in Jesus it took on unequivocal and uncompromising character. Jesus resembled the Pharisees through and through in his understanding that man owed to God perfect obedience. But he renewed and completed radically and decisively the prophetic revolution by freeing the understanding of God's will from the archaic elements with which it had been entangled.

Jesus' transformation of his Jewish heritage went far beyond this. That love of God and neighbor were the chief among the requirements of God had long been known. Yet the understanding of the meaning of these requirements had always been bound up with the practice of the whole law. The law of love was the most important among the laws, and in announcing it as such Jesus added nothing new. But Pharisaic Judaism, while recognizing the supreme importance of love, had not reinterpreted the whole relation of God and man in terms of love. Rather, it had interpreted the commandment of love in the context of the law, and this had led to hedging the application of the law about with numerous qualifications. Here, too, Jesus crossed a threshold and thus transformed the meaning of the materials that he took with him across the threshold. For him, love demanded an unselfseeking openness to the need of the neighbor, and this neighbor was any man who was in need. No traditional law that interfered with the immediate and responsible expression of that love could be allowed to stand.

The understanding of love was transformed also in another respect. For both Jesus and the Pharisees, love was a matter both of action and of inner intention. Yet the relation between these altered in Jesus. For the Pharisees, the commands of God included the demand for purity of motive and purpose as well as righteousness of action. But these commands, like those which we could distinguish as ethical and ritual, lay side by side. Jesus attached a radical priority to the inner state. Since love was no longer to be expressed by obedience to many principles, it had to be a matter of the heart. Even righteous acts were worthless in God's sight if they were not motivated by love.

This leads to another striking point of contrast between Jesus and the Pharisees. The Pharisees lived in a more or less stable world ruled by God but from which God was somewhat remote. In this context, they had to discover the will of God for each new problem as it arose. This they did by application of the old law. In each case, the law must be so interpreted as to designate some possible course of action as right. Hence, what was demanded must be a practical act within the power of man to effect.

Jesus lived in a world that had no permanence and to which God was very near. In such a world, the question of what was to be done was not settled by the capacities of man or the probable consequences for society. What was demanded was determined by what God was and the meaning of what God was for human life.

As long as the ethical demand was assumed to lie fully within the power of man to obey, it could deal only with behavior rather than with motives. To command that motives be pure was to command the impossible. But this did not matter to Jesus. In the white heat generated by the nearness of God, intentions also must and could be pure.

The possibility of such purity belonged with the understanding of God's grace. Alongside the absolute radicalization and interiorization of the ethical demand stood the radicalization of trust in God. What a person asked of God confidently, he received. God was far more eager to give than man was open to accept. Indeed, God in his love was already and especially seeking the sinner.

At this point, too, the Pharisaic ethical consciousness was radically transcended. The Pharisee knew that God's justice was tempered with mercy. God would forgive the penitent if he turned to righteousness. But mercy should operate within the context of justice. The conditions for salvation were established by God, and man had to adapt himself to them.

For Jesus, on the other hand, the whole radical demand of God on men was placed in the context of God's love. Men were not to think of objective conditions that they must try to meet, but of the active initiative of God coming to them and offering them the Kingdom. God sought out the sinner while he was sinner. Jesus asked, in the first place, only openness or receptivity. Such openness and receptivity, he found more frequently among those who knew themselves as sinners than among the outwardly righteous members of society. Hence, the whole hierarchy of evaluations based upon law and obedience was overturned as the initiative was seen to be in the hands of the loving Father rather than with the ethical striving of man.

The difference can also be stated in terms of freedom. For the Pharisee, the individual man was free to *do* or not to do what God required of him. For Jesus, the individual man was free to *be* or not to be what God wanted him to be. Of course, for the Pharisee and Jesus alike, what one was and what one did were inseparable. But whereas for the Pharisee one was what one did, for Jesus one acted in terms of what one was. The freedom to *be* what one willed to be was a far greater freedom, and hence also a far greater burden, than the freedom to *do* what one wanted to do.

The resurrection appearances of Jesus created a community of intense excitement and expectancy. In part, they directed this community back to the sayings and deeds of Jesus in which he had given expression to his own existence. But more directly, they constituted for the community the powerful evidence that the old aeon was truly broken and that God had drawn near. The community came into existence in a rejoicing over the resurrection as given reality and in expectation of its imminent universalization. In the excitement of this faith, the effective presence of God was vividly known.

Despite the similarity of the belief and experience of the early Christians with that of Jesus himself, there was also an important difference. For Jesus, the belief in the imminence of the Kingdom was a function of the experiential knowledge of the immediacy of God. He encouraged his hearers to enter into an interpersonal relation with God in perfect trust. For the early Christians, on the other hand, it was what God had done in Jesus' resurrection that opened them to God in confident expectation of what God would do. Almost as a by-product of this belief, they found themselves open to the present work of God in their lives. This present work was experienced more as an empowering presence than as a Thou who was heard and addressed.

This new relation to God found expression in a new terminology. Jesus had spoken very little of the divine Spirit. Like the great prophets of the eighth century, he may have avoided this language quite consciously. In that earlier period, the Spirit of God had been associated with ecstatic possession. When the Spirit came upon a person, he lost his individual conscious center; he became a passive and non-responsible instrument for God to speak or act through. Where the prophet thought of himself as an individual addressed by God, who then communicated the divine message to his people, he eschewed the idea of Spirit possession. He was involved in a relationship as person with the personal God.

But in the life of the primitive Christian community, the Spirit played a central role. Men experienced themselves as under the influence of divine power that acted in and through their total psyche. God was known as empowering presence at least as clearly as he was known as Heavenly Father. So important was this experience in the self-understanding of the Christian community, that we can use it as a basis for understanding the peculiarity of that existence generally.

Our first question must be to what extent the recurrence of the phenomenon of the Spirit implies a return to archaic patterns of religion. To some degree and in some instances, it must have meant just that and has meant that again and again in Christian history in revivals of the pneumatic emphasis. Speaking in tongues, ecstatic prophesying, and other phenomena seem to have occurred that involve surrender of the conscious center of personality to forces which operate from or through the unconscious.

Furthermore, this is not simply to be deplored. The magnificent attainments of the axial period and the resulting transformations of the structures of human existence command our admiration and deserve our gratitude. Yet we must not hide from ourselves the extremely precarious character of that achievement. Since consciousness is, in fact, so small a part of the total psychic life, its struggle to wrest control and determine the meanings by which life is to be lived is always a struggle against immense odds. The attainment of rational and ethical existence in Greece and Israel required also a great suppression or repression of psychic forces. The unconscious was controlled but not itself transformed or even understood. Axial existence requires a continual psychic effort and discipline that is extremely demanding and often inhibits the spontaneities of mutual affection and acceptance.

In the eschatological Christian community, the sense that the structures of communal and individual existence which had governed the past were now already at an end may well have relaxed the guard of consciousness against the powers of the unconscious. When this happened, there was a sense of release and refreshment, the possibility of feeling whole and at peace. There was also a release of paranormal powers leading to extraordinary results that were highly prized.

The revival of the archaic experience of the divine Spirit involved the danger that the personal reality of man and the understanding of God as personal would be destroyed. The I–Thou relation to God characteristic of Israel might be replaced by an I-it relation in which, as Buber has taught us, the " I " also loses its personal character. In such an I-it relation, the " I " could be either God or man. When the Holy Spirit was seen as initiating agent, man might appear as a passive instrument. When man assumed the role of actor, he might try to manipulate the Spirit as an impersonal force.

Despite the dangers of reversion to archaic existence given with the new prominence of the experience of the Spirit, such reversion was rejected by the mainstream of Christianity. The church attained an understanding of the work of the Holy Spirit in which the Hebrew axial achievement was affirmed and carried farther. Paul interpreted the indwelling, empowering, and transforming Spirit as personal Spirit interacting with human personal spirit. Furthermore, he saw the essential and characteristic fruit of the presence of the Holy Spirit not in ecstatic phenomena but in a transformation of the quality of the reflective consciousness itself. He saw in the Spirit a pervasive power working continually within the Christian to produce peace, joy, patience, humility, and love.

Although the personal character of the I–Thou relation between man and God was thus preserved, what resulted in the Christian experience of the Holy Spirit was not what is usually meant by the I–Thou relation, for that relation suggests overagainstness, confrontation, speech, and response. The relation of the primitive Christian believer to the Spirit was far more intimate than that. There was no imagery of spatial separation or of demand and obedience. There was, rather, the imagery of two spiritual realities, each fully responsible for itself and self-identical, nevertheless mutually indwelling each other.

Whether this personal presence indwelling the believer was thought of as the Spirit or as Christ or as God in some other form does not really matter. To us the conceptual problem is acutely posed. But as we attempt to understand the character of Christian existence in the primitive community, the decisive point is that the personal God was known as inwardly present without loss of the sense of responsible personhood. Indeed, God was known as inwardly present in such a way as to enhance and accentuate the sense of personhood.

In the preceding paragraphs, the term " spirit " has been used repeatedly to refer to the human spirit. It has been used without precise definition and in a way that hardly distinguishes it from my use of person. This nontechnical use of spirit is also characteristic of the New Testament. The Christian community did not have the philosopher's concern for terminological precision, and even Paul uses his major anthropological terms in ways that are often interchangeable. " Spirit " can mean the self, the soul, attitude, or will. Probably all its meanings reflect uses that are independent of the prophetic understanding of man.

Nevertheless, this term is here selected to designate the new element in Christian existence. This use of the term receives general support from the New Testament, and is also in accord with one of the meanings widely given to it in contemporary usage. In what follows, " spirit " refers to the radically self-transcending character of human existence that emerged in the Christian community. In this sense, spiritual existence is a further development of personal existence.

In the last chapter, personhood was defined in terms of the individual's acceptance of responsibility for himself and his awareness of his inwardness. As personhood emerged in Israel, it formed itself in a way that we find natural to designate by human will.[21] Hebrew

[21] This term is needed here and below to distinguish the seat of personal existence from that of spiritual existence. As indicated in note 19, it is an appropriate designation of this seat only when it has been transcended, for " will " suggests at least the possibility of its distinction from the self or " I."

man knew himself as one who confronted a choice and was responsible for his voluntary decision. In deciding on the course of action, he was deciding on what he was to be. To us it is surprising that a term more clearly equivalent to our idea of the will is not far more prominent in the Hebrew scriptures. Perhaps the more encompassing concept of " heart " tended to be understood centrally as what we would call " will." In any case, we can largely understand prophetic man in terms of two factors: the total physical, social, and historical context in which he lived and his personal will as that by which he transcended that context and determined the form his life would take within it.

For the primitive Christian community, a new dimension appeared. Attention was focused to a much greater degree on the psychic state as such rather than only on outward action. This psychic state took on great importance both because, as prophetic Judaism already knew, God looked on the heart, and also because the inner man was the seat of the presence and activity of God's Spirit. Outward behavior was understood to flow forth from the heart and to reflect its total state. Also, Christian belief or faith, unlike Pharisaic obedience, was initially a matter of an inner state rather than of observable conduct.

This attention to the inwardness of man greatly complicated the understanding of personal responsibility as focused in the will. As long as responsibility was primarily for voluntary actions, man must be seen as able, in a quite simple and direct sense, to do what he ought. But when actions were seen in terms of motives and attention was directed toward the motive rather than to the act, such an uncomplicated understanding of responsibility led to immense difficulties. Perhaps Jesus' own understanding retained this straightforward sense of the possibility of obedience, but certainly in the experience of the Christian community it could not endure. On the one hand, man *ought* to have a pure heart, to act only from love of God and neighbor. On the other hand, he found all sorts of resistances in himself to such action. He wanted to overcome these resistances, yet they remained. Were they then elements alien to himself for which he had no responsibility? One could not quite say that, for they were too intimately a part of the self, even affecting the willing itself. There seemed to be a power of sin in man's life that was not simply subject to his will and yet was bound up with that will. If man was to become genuinely righteous and not merely to conform his outward action to approved patterns, he must be aided from outside his own resources. Indeed, he was wholly dependent on the divine initiative.

One might suppose that the sense of dependence on the divine initiative would lead to a reduced sense of personal responsibility. But this did not occur. The Christian experienced himself as radically responsible for himself beyond the point of his actual apparent ability to choose. Here is the seat of the rationally perplexing but existentially powerful understanding of original sin, a notion almost wholly lacking in Judaism but pervasively effective in Christianity, even where its verbalization is repudiated. Somehow, the Christian knew himself as responsible for choosing to be the kind of self he was, even when he found that his desire to change himself into another kind of self was ineffectual. Hence, he must shift his efforts from a direct struggle to alter himself to the attempt to become open to the work of the divine Spirit that could do within him something which he could not do in and for himself. Even here he knew that his very opening of himself toward God depended on God's initiative and that this opening, in its turn, was very fragmentary indeed.

The Christian had to accept a responsibility for his existence as a whole in a way that separated him from Judaism. This meant that he must understand himself as transcending his will in the sense of his power of choice among practicable alternatives in a given situation. He was responsible not only for his choice but also for the motive of his choosing. He was responsible for being the kind of self who could not will to choose to have the motive he should.

In principle, we can press this responsibility ad infinitum. At whatever level we ask the question about what we are, we also must acknowledge our responsibility for being that. We cannot simply accept what we are as the given context within which our responsibility operates. If I find that I am not a loving person, I must acknowledge my responsibility for not being a loving person; and if I find that I cannot even will to become a loving person, I must acknowledge responsibility for that failure of my will. I cannot identify myself with some one aspect of my total psyche, some one force within it. If with the Jew I identify myself with the will, then I know myself as responsible for that self-identification and hence as transcending it. Even more, if with many of the Greeks I identify myself with reason, I know that I am responsible for that choice and hence transcend the reason with which I have identified myself.

Of course, this sort of analysis is not present in the New Testament texts. They expressed only a relatively early stage of the development of this self-conscious self-transcendence. Attention was focused away from the self, its acts and self-consciousness, toward the work of God in Jesus Christ and in the Holy Spirit and toward the consummation so soon to come. The practical problems of organizing life in the present were dealt with only as the needs were insistent.

Although the emphasis thus far has been placed on responsibility, in the New Testament the work of the Spirit is known much more as freedom. Man was free from the law, because he could live immediately from the grace that was the Spirit. He did not need to struggle to obey imposed principles of conduct, because his heart was changed. Those principles were now either set aside as irrelevant or accepted as the spontaneous expression of the new heart that he found within himself as the work of the Spirit. Man was free from his own past, because the Spirit placed him on a new level of existence in which that past had no power over him. Man was free from the oppressive powers of this world, the structures within the context of which he had understood his existence, because he now lived in terms of a reality that radically transcended and relativized them. He knew Christian existence, therefore, as joy rather than as burden.

In the New Testament, we see a stage of development in which the primacy of the Holy Spirit was so great in the understanding of Christian existence that there was simply no place for using the gifts of the Spirit wrongly. That one should use the freedom granted by the Spirit for immorality was unintelligible, although, of course, even then it occurred. The New Testament had not yet reached the understanding of spiritual sins.

The church, however, came rapidly enough to recognize that the existence of man as spirit was by no means an insurance of virtue. It introduced man to a new level of sin as well as to new possibilities of self-sacrificial love. Spiritual existence has brought into human history depths of both good and evil that are impossible in any other context. The finest achievements of man and his most hideous crimes are alike spiritual acts.

That the emergence of spiritual existence is the emergence of enhanced possibilities for both good and evil is nothing new. The same could be said for personal existence and, indeed, for axial existence in general, or of civilized existence, or, before that, of human existence as such. This means, however, that we cannot simply identify prophetic existence with personal existence or Christian existence with spiritual existence. Prophetic existence is personal existence that exercises its personal responsibility in trust and obedience. Christian existence is spiritual existence that exercises its new freedom in love. The nature of this love and the way it fulfills spiritual existence are the chief topics of the next chapter.

Personal existence is that structure of existence realized in prophetic Judaism, and spiritual existence is the new structure that emerged in the primitive Christian community. In concluding this chapter, a direct description of this structure is needed.

In personal existence, a center emerged in the conscious psyche that transcended such impersonal forces as passion and reason, which were operative therein, and experienced responsibility for their mutual relations. From the perspective of spiritual existence, this center can be identified with the will.

In spiritual existence, a new level of transcendence appeared. The self became responsible for the choice of the center from which it organized itself and not only for what it chose from a given center. If it chose to identify itself as will and to accept the bondage to moral obligation that was therein entailed, it could do so. But it need not do so, and it should not do so. If it did do so, it was responsible for this choice as well as for the further choices that it made as will.

If it is difficult to conceptualize the structure of *personal* existence, the difficulty is compounded when we come to spiritual existence. Here we must think of a reflective consciousness in which the seat of existence is capable of changing. Furthermore, we must think of this changing center as itself responsible for this changing, and thus transcendent of the locus from which it organizes the whole. Finally, we must conceive this transcendent center as capable of retaining its transcendent identity and of refusing to identify itself with any other aspect of the psyche. Obviously, as long as we derive our images from visual sources, such a *concept* is impossible. Yet, it fits the facts of experience as expressed in much Christian literature and can be confirmed by many in their own self-understanding.

The spiritual structure of existence resulted from an intensification and radicalization of that responsibility for oneself which is the mark also of personal existence. If a person accepts responsibility for his action and recognizes that this requires his control over his emotions and thought, then by that act he becomes an "I" that transcends his emotions and thought. The emergence of that "I" marks the advent of personal existence. But the personal "I" cannot be responsible for what it cannot control. It cannot be responsible for the occurrence of particular emotions, only for channeling them into righteous action. It cannot be responsible for the limits of its own capacity. It cannot be responsible for itself as it is given to itself. Thus, the "I" of personal existence transcends every other element in the reflective consciousness, but it does not transcend itself.

The message of Jesus, on the one hand, and the experience of the Holy Spirit, on the other, broke through this last barrier to total responsibility. The essential demand of God has to do precisely with those dimensions of selfhood which the personal "I" cannot control. To accept those demands and to accept responsibility to live in terms of them is to accept radical responsibility for oneself, and that is, at the same time, to transcend one's self. That means that the new spiritual "I" is responsible both for what it is and for what it is not, both for what lies in its power and for what lies beyond its power. For the spiritual "I" need not remain itself but can, instead, always transcend itself. Thus, spiritual existence is radically self-transcending existence.

Chapter Eleven

LOVE

In the last chapter, Christian existence was defined as spiritual existence that expresses itself in love. Spiritual existence was then explained as a structure of radical self-transcendence, and its power for both good and evil was emphasized. Yet no explanation was given as to what that love is by virtue of which the peculiar ideal of Christianity is embodied and fulfilled. Is Christian love to be understood as identical with a universal human phenomenon that is in turn continuous with the affection animals show for one another and for men? Or is Christian love something discontinuous from all other forms of love such that a distinct word is needed? In either case, why does love play so central a role for Christian existence, whereas other forms of existence can be more or less adequately treated without special reference to it? To answer these questions, it will be necessary to discuss what is meant by love in the very broadest sense, and then to compare the form love took in the several axial cultures.

In an extremely loose sense, it can be said that every entity loves itself and other entities. That is, every entity is something for itself as subject and perceives the world from this perspective. Everything is appraised in terms of its capacity to contribute to the richness of this momentary experience, which is prized for its own sake. At the same time, every entity has some concern for the future, that is, for other entities still to come; and in its self-actualization, it so constitutes itself as to contribute to that future. In this very general sense, the Whiteheadian philosophy (by which I am so greatly influenced) affirms " self-love " and " other-love " of every entity whatsoever.

Such an ontological context is useful for the understanding of love, but it is better to use the term "love" for something much more limited. Ordinarily, we first apply the word at the level of the animal world. We describe especially sexual attraction and the concern of mother animals for their young as love, and occasionally we observe among animals additional relations to which we spontaneously apply the word "love." We say, for example, that a dog loves its master. But for the most part, the relations in question appear to be instinctive, that is, determined by organic structures other than the animal soul.

The whole presentation in this book has emphasized continuities — also the continuity between animal and human existence. Such continuity exists also between animal and human love. There are noninstinctive elements in animal love, and there are instinctive elements in human love. But among men, love is importantly a function of the autonomous activity of the psyche. The extensive importance of this noninstinctive love in human beings emerged very gradually through human development. Nevertheless, a threshold was crossed, and human love must be understood on its own terms.

When we limit our attention to human, noninstinctive love, we still have before us an exceedingly complex phenomenon. Much noninstinctive love is unconsciously determined. Needs and desires unknown to our conscious minds control the direction and form of our affection and desire. This is especially clear in the whole area of sexual attraction, in which conscious interests seem to be overwhelmingly governed by unconscious needs. A man who identifies himself with his consciousness often perceives his sexual passions as an alien force with which he must come to terms, rather than as fully part of his very self. When we realize how large a role our sexuality plays in the whole of our lives, the importance of the unconscious element in human love is impressive. Nevertheless, although unconsciously controlled love is of great power in all human life, the love that emerged into importance in the axial period was an activity of consciousness.

Before the several forms of conscious love can be treated, a methodological problem must be considered. If we were comparing sexual attraction in the several cultures, there would be a biological and instinctual common factor that would enable us to display the variety of expressions as expressions of one thing. But love in this noninstinctual, conscious sense has no such common factor. Also, there is not some one word in each language self-evidently equivalent with "love," such that we could study its applications in each case and thus succeed in our comparison. Instead, the decision as to what our question is must be made first in much more general terms, and only then can we institute a comparison.

In what follows, then, I shall mean by "love" any mode of relating to an object as a positive intrinsic value,[22] in which conscious psychic activity is decisively involved. By "object" here I do not mean a mere thing in contrast to a person, but rather an intentional or epistemological object, which can be either personal or impersonal. In the relation of love, the separation of the lover and the beloved may be overcome, but when no such separation initially exists, it is not appropriate to speak of love. Love requires some distinction between the subject and the object. Even in the case of self-love this is true. The newborn infant is completely selfish from the point of view of an adult, but it does not love itself. To love oneself requires some notion of oneself as one among the entities of the world, singled out for special concern. It becomes possible only when there is some measure of self-awareness, that is, only when the self becomes an object to itself.

On the basis of this understanding of love as positive valuation of an object, we can distinguish four types of love among the Greeks. There was, first, desire. This was attending to the object as that which provided satisfactions to the subject. Its goal was possession. The object of such love might be inanimate things, or it might be something abstract, such as prestige, success, or power. It might, of course, be an object, the possession of which yielded sexual pleasure.

Second, there was adoration. Rather than seeking to possess an object because of the pleasure or satisfaction it yielded to the subject, the subject surrendered itself to the object. Such surrender might afford a certain kind of pleasure, but in this case the pleasure came from being possessed rather than from possessing. Such adoration might

[22] I am here opposing intrinsic value to instrumental value. That is, in love one relates to something for its own sake and not only as an instrument to some further goal. That one so relates does not exclude the possibility that the value is a product of the love rather than its independent condition.

be directed toward another person or toward deity or even toward an abstraction.

Desire and adoration as such are universal. Among primitive peoples, they were largely or entirely functions of instinctive or unconscious psychic needs. Instinctive and unconscious elements continued prominent among axial peoples, but these forms of love could also contain a large element of autonomous conscious activity. A third type of love, aesthetic admiration, was more distinctively Greek and reflected the triumph of consciousness more clearly.

In aesthetic admiration, there was no attempt either to gain possession of the object for the subject or to surrender the subject to the possession of the object. Rather, the subject remained subject and the object remained object. The subject was open to the perfection of form in the object and enjoyed it as such, without either desire or adoration. The distance of the aesthetic experience was maintained. Such a relation was possible not only toward objects of art but also toward human beings, in terms either of their physical beauty or of their excellence of character and action.

Fourth, there was friendship. This differed from the others in that it could only be between human beings and must involve mutuality. Furthermore, because it was directed toward another individual it could involve the desire for his good, and in its truest forms it had to do so. However, in other respects, friendship was not independent in its nature from other forms of love. A friendship might be based either on the respective desires of the friends, as each brought satisfaction to the other, or on admiration of the excellence of one another's character and action.

Self-love was not a category of Greek experience and reflection alongside other forms of love. This was because Greek thought took for granted that each man wanted the good for himself. The question was not whether this was or was not an acceptable motivation for action, but rather what constituted the good and how it was to be obtained. Even in Aristotle's discussion of friendship, where he made very clear that one could and should wish other men well quite apart from the advantage that accrued to the well-wisher, he also affirmed that there might be limits to this well-wishing since, of course, every man, above all, wishes himself well. Furthermore, the entire discussion of friendship is found in the context of an analysis of how man achieves happiness. The reason for having friends, even where friendship included disinterested well-wishing, was that it was a part of the good life in which alone man found his happiness.

There were those among the Greeks who saw in love of all these kinds a threat to happiness. Concern for an object, whether that be desire for possession, aesthetic appreciation, or even a will for its benefit, placed a person at the mercy of forces he could not control. It subjected him to the pain of loss and disappointment. Hence, in later Greek thought, apathy, which included the absence of love in all these senses, was a much approved state of mind.

At one level, this constitutes a point of contact with Indian thought. There one might well argue that freedom from love was very much the goal. This is true, if love is understood in any of the senses outlined above. Indeed, the profound psychological analyses of the Indians went farther than this.

The Indian was conscious of his own seat of existence in a way largely lacking among the Greeks. Hence, he knew that it was possible to attach himself to this seat in its particularity and individuality, and to attempt to maintain and enhance his separate selfhood. This self-love might constitute a subtler and more dangerous obstacle to the attainment of release than even attachment to other things and persons. It could be prevented only by the realization that the seat of existence is not the true self.

On the other hand, at least in some of its Buddhist forms, Indian thought attained a very exalted conception of love. This love is both so important and so difficult for the Western mind to understand that we must pause briefly to reflect on it.

We have seen earlier that the Buddhist both dissolved the structuring of the world, which is caused by concepts, and overcame the unification of successive occasions of human experience, which is the product of self-identification with past and future. All that remained were discrete and ever-perishing congeries of elements.

However, later Buddhism carried its negation even farther. Primitive Buddhism sought to extinguish desire, and thus also suffering, through the denial of any eminent reality and through the analysis of reality into a flux of elements. But the status of these ever-perishing elements was itself problematic. Primitive Buddhism had already denied their substantiality and permanence, but the Madhyamika school denied also their reality, thus completing the metaphysical dissolution of reality. This dissolution paved the way for the reinstitution of Reality in the sense of an intuitively and mystically apprehended undifferentiated unity.[23]

The denial of reality applied to the human occasions of experience as well. Thus the goal of life became not merely the overcoming of projection of human meanings on the world and of identity with past and future, but, more radically, an overcoming of all distinction and all differentiation. The total emptying of consciousness necessary to such an attainment would seem to the Westerner to lead to total indifference to the phenomenal world. Surprisingly, it did not. In Mahayana Buddhism, alongside the quest for release arose the ideal of compassion supremely symbolized in the Boddhisattva, who renounced Nirvana itself for the sake of bringing enlightenment to an ignorant world.

Compassion was the opposite of desire. Desire was the longing of some subject for some attainment or possession for itself. It presupposed, therefore, a differentiated world. Insofar as one realized the unity in the voidness of all things, desire was impossible and was replaced by total openness to all things and undifferentiated goodwill.

Strictly speaking, ideal compassion was not conceived as a form of love according to the definition of love in this chapter, for in it there was ultimately no distinction of subject and object of love. Nevertheless, its normal description and practice presuppose such a distinction. The Boddhisattva loved all things, and thus the subject-object structure appeared. But since there is finally no Boddhisattva " self," and since all things are equally himself, the dualism was overcome.

In describing the place of love in Greek and Indian existence, it has been possible to omit reference to man's love for God. For the Greeks, the gods might be aesthetically admired or even adored, and for Aristotle the contemplation of God was the highest good. But the love of God remained one of many aspects of the excellent life. For India, the

---

[23] In this discussion of later Buddhism, especially the Madhyamika school, I have been chiefly influenced by Thomas Altizer, *Oriental Mysticism and Biblical Eschatology* (The Westminster Press, 1961), pp. 132 ff.

holy power could take personal form, and believing adoration or loving devotion toward the deity was widely practiced. Nevertheless,
bhakti was but one of several ways in which man could or should relate himself to Brahman or to one of the Buddhas in some later forms
of Buddhism. For the Hebrews, in contrast, the love of God was the
central form of love and the determining principle of all life.

Love of God was the acknowledgment of what he was in his in-
commensurate superiority in relation to man. Because God was understood primarily as will, the acknowledgment of what he was was
primarily obedience. The love that was commanded as the sum of the
law was obedient love, the willing conformity of life to his will.

It is extremely difficult to say whether prophetic man loved God
for God's sake or for his own sake. Often the expected motivation
was desire for one's own advantage, and obedience was required because of God's power to reward and punish. Nevertheless, this would
be a very one-sided view of the situation. Prophetic man was not
first committed to calculating self-interest and then persuaded that he
could achieve his interests best by obedience to God. Obedience to
God was right because God was who he was, because of what he had
done for Israel in the past, and because of his loving-kindness to Israel. Obedience was all the more right, because God was a just God
who dealt with men mercifully, yet according to their deserts. Since
what was right and what was advantageous were identical, the issue
of their relation rarely arose clearly. Yet it did arise, and when this
happened, the Hebrew knew that he must serve God even at personal
cost and apart from expectation of reward.

That this question could arise at all points to a distinctive aspect of
Hebrew love. Among the Greeks and even among the Indians, that
the ultimate reference of concern is oneself was not in question. But
where the I–Thou relation was clearly present, this question did arise.
There were two persons involved, the human and the divine, and man
recognized that love could be directed toward either. A person might
be concerned only for himself and interested in the other only as
means to his own ends, or he might actually be concerned about the
other to such a point as to be willing to sacrifice his own ends. Thus,
there arose a distinction of immense importance between love of the
other and love of self.

The other was initially and primarily God, and in this relation, the love of the other must take ultimate precedence. However, the love of God as person transformed also man's relation to his fellowman. In preaxial culture, this relation had been one of solidarity governed by principles of give and take. It had always included elements of spontaneous affection and generosity. But in that context, the question of the right balance of concern for self and concern for the neighbor did not arise. Even among the Greeks, we have seen, concern for the neighbor was treated within the context of presupposed primary concern for self. Despite highly developed individuality, and the capacity to distance himself as one individual among others, man's natural self-centeredness as such did not come into question. This could occur only where the other as person could demand personal devotion, even at the cost of personal satisfaction — and that happened only in Israel. Once it had happened in relation to God, the question of the right relation between man and man arose in a quite new way. Self-centeredness was no longer simply given. The deeper reality of all things was to be found in God's perception of the world, and in that perception, each person was only one among others. Hence, the genuinely appropriate relation to one's neighbor and to oneself was the same. One should love one's neighbor as oneself.

The demand for equal love of neighbor expressed the situation of personal existence before the personal God. The love that was demanded was a matter both of motivation and of outward action. A person must seek the good of the neighbor for the neighbor's sake, just as he sought his own good for his own sake. Nevertheless, the demand was addressed to the person as will and was a demand for that which the will could fulfill. Hence, it was not to be interpreted as a challenge to the natural and inevitable self-centeredness of man's feelings. If a man willfully sought his own benefit at the expense of his neighbor, he was guilty of violating the commandment of love. But whether, when he acted justly, he was really concerned for the neighbor's good, rather than for his own righteousness, was hardly a serious consideration.

Prophetic man transcended himself in that he could see himself as one object of love alongside others. But the impartial love required of him must be a love of which he was capable in the free exercise of his will. In Christianity, this limitation was broken through. The same commandments of love of God and love of neighbor remained. But the meaning was transformed. Love was understood as a motive, a state of feeling giving rise to willing and to acting. Thus, what was commanded or required came into conflict for the first time with man's natural self-centeredness of feeling. Even if he went far beyond all reasonable demands of self-sacrifice in favor of the neighbor, even if he gave all his goods to feed the poor, he must recognize that this might not express the requisite attitude or inner state. But then, the love that was required was no longer under the control of the will. In the last chapter, the connection of the radical demand for love with the primacy of grace and the sense of original sin was discussed. The remainder of this chapter is devoted to a discussion of the reason for the necessity of this love for the fulfillment of spiritual existence.

Love has importance in every tradition. Especially in Israel, it is clear, love to God and fellowman was central to the law as a whole. Nevertheless, that which was commanded in these laws could be almost equally well expressed by the commands of obedience and justice. Only in Christianity did love as something transcending such obedience and justice become in itself the fulfillment of all that was required. This means not only that the love involved was something new, but also that the need for such love was now unlimited.

Each of us perceives the whole of reality from his own limited standpoint and evaluates it in terms of its contribution to himself. At the same time, he feels spontaneous concern for others, independently of their contribution to his own welfare. He can and does experience admiration, devotion, affection, and sympathy. It is not helpful at this level to ask whether this spontaneous love of the other constitutes altruism in contrast to self-interest. When a person acts on behalf of someone who has won his sympathy, the welfare of the other person has become *his* interest — it is a new self-interest altered by the genuine concern for the welfare of the other. Self-interest and altruism merge unproblematically.

Insofar, however, as the self objectifies itself as one self among others, its relations with other selves cease to be simply and naïvely spontaneous. Among axial peoples, there was judgment about proper and ideal relations with others, and this created critical self-consciousness about one's immediate impulses and feelings. But as long as the basic self-centeredness of feeling was taken for granted, man's primary attention could be directed away from himself toward others and toward his relations to them. Natural self-centeredness and spontaneous concern for others remained.

However, in spiritual existence, man objectified and experienced responsibility for his basic self-centeredness of feeling. He judged this against the norm of genuine love of God and neighbor and found it corrupt and corrupting. Furthermore, the transcendence of the spirit over itself meant that man was not simply bound to the primacy of self-regard. Yet the judgment against self-centeredness and the awareness of self-transcendence did not lessen the power of self-centeredness. Instead, they heightened it and transformed it from a mere fact into sin. A self-centeredness that was simply given and that attended to the things of its world became a self-preoccupation that cut off the possibility of healthy openness to others. The self could manipulate all a man's relations with other selves, even his feelings about them and their feelings about him, for his own sake, and it could do so consciously and willfully.

This self-preoccupation is spiritual pride. This word is not to be narrowly understood. In its narrow use, " pride " may be juxtaposed to modesty or humility as two modes of personal bearing. Or pride may be understood as having a high opinion of oneself and one's abilities. In these senses, pride is a limited and manageable problem and even has much to commend it. Self-centeredness in the self-conscious man can manifest itself in these ways, or in self-aggrandizement at the expense of others. But it can equally well, and perhaps more insidiously, manifest itself in self-pity, self-condemnation, and fearfulness. These are all alike forms of self-preoccupation.

It is no wonder that the radical self-transcendence that leads to self-preoccupation is sometimes regarded as a sickness. It does disrupt and distort the spontaneous and healthy relations possible to those who live unselfconsciously. What is required if this sickness is to be escaped at the level of spirit is a genuine concern for the other that is free from self-regard. That is, the vicious circle of self-preoccupation is broken only when a person loves others without regard to the effect of that love on himself. That means that he loves others without regard to the fact that only by such love can he break out of his self-enclosedness. But every effort to love, in order to break out of the misery of self-preoccupation, is also an expression of the self-preoccupation and is condemned to intensify it.

Love is, therefore, on the one hand, the only salvation of the spiritual man and, on the other hand, unattainable by his own efforts. The spiritual man can only love when he is freed from the necessity to love, that is, when he knows himself already loved in his self-preoccupation. Only if man finds that he is already accepted in his sin and sickness, can he accept his own self-preoccupation as it is; and only then can his psychic economy be opened toward others, to accept them as they are — not in order to save himself, but because he doesn't need to save himself. We love only because we are first loved. In this way, and only in this way, can the spiritual man genuinely and purely love.

This discussion of love has illustrated the greater extremes of both evil and good that appear at the level of spirit. On the one hand lies the corruption of spontaneous feeling by self-preoccupation or pride. On the other hand lies the possibility of Christian love — a love that uniquely transcends self-centeredness in a genuine concern for the other, untainted by concern for its consequences for the lover.

No Christian should lay claim to any simple embodiment of such love. In the totality of his relations to any person, he must recognize a great complexity of feeling — instinctual, unconscious, and self-seeking. Nevertheless, the whole can be, and often is, redeemed by the presence of an element of genuine concern for the other as a person.

One peculiarity of Christian love is its independence of the merits of the one who is loved. So long as the self-centeredness of human interest in the world was unquestioned, love as motive had to be evoked by some property of the object loved or by some property unconsciously projected on it. Men could love only what presented itself to them as lovable. When love was commanded, as in Israel, it could no longer be a matter of love as motive. The effective motive of obedience to such a command was the desire to be righteous rather than the concern for the other as another.

But for the Christian, love is the possibility of openness to the other as another and concern for him as such. It is made possible by the gift of an undeserved love, and hence it cannot seek a deserving object for its expression. The possibility of its occurrence consists in a freedom from the sickness of self-preoccupation, and, hence, the prior relation of the other to the self cannot be relevant.

In Christian love, we are free from bondage to ourselves without ceasing to be the self-transcending selves of spiritual existence. Lover and loved retain their full personal, responsible autonomy. Love imposes no demand on the one loved; it seeks, rather, his freedom. There is no merging of self and other, as in the love of desire and adoration.

Christian love saves spiritual man from the sickness of self-preoccupation, but this does not imply that it leads to euphoria. Openness to the other is openness to his sin and suffering as well as to his joy, and that means that love brings pain. At a certain level, love greatly increases the suffering of the lover. There has always been in the world a vast amount of human suffering, and to love one's fellowmen means that this suffering must constantly be a part of one's own experience. But this suffering does not destroy the sufferer as does the suffering of self-preoccupation. Instead, if he does not flinch from it, but rather continues to love, his capacity for love increases, and his suffering can be accompanied by a deeper peace and joy.

Here we touch on a part of the innermost mystery of Christian existence, the many-faceted truth that only he who loses his soul can find it. It is a truth that all of us find repeatedly confirmed in our own existence, and in which, yet, we have only the most fragmentary participation.

Chapter Twelve

THE QUESTION OF FINALITY

At the beginning of this book, the questions of the distinctiveness of Christianity and its finality were distinguished. It was argued that the former should be treated in some abstraction from the latter before the latter could be appropriately considered. Hence, in most of the book different forms of existence have been presented with only incidental attention to comparative evaluations. In this concluding chapter, however, it is appropriate to reflect on the Christian claim that Christianity is not only distinctive but also in an important sense final.

The Christian perspective from which this book is written has been apparent throughout in the selection and organization of the material. Nevertheless, the descriptions of the several structures of existence aim at a degree of objectivity in the sense that their relative accuracy should be subject to evaluation also from other perspectives. When the question of evaluation is raised, and "finality" is chiefly an evaluative category, the dominance of the perspective increases. Hence, in this chapter I must speak more explicitly as a Christian concerned with the intelligibility and credibility of the Christian claim to finality. This does not mean that I am made confident of this claim through some suprarational act of faith. The Christian claim is a problematical one to me, as it is to many Christians, and the years of reflection that lie behind the present formulation might, so far as I am consciously aware, have led to much more relativistic conclusions. But the concern for *this* claim rather than some other is determined by a Christian perspective, and the persuasiveness of the arguments which convince me that it has some measure of validity depends in part on that perspective.

We must consider, first, for what the Christian claims finality. The answer is Jesus Christ. Furthermore, the Christian may make this claim on grounds that this book has not touched; for example, on the grounds that in Jesus and only in him God became man. Discussion of that kind of claim cannot be undertaken here. The claim may also be made, however, in terms of the work of Christ, and this work may be considered historically. The previous chapters have prepared the way for reconsideration of this form of claim.

If we consider the work of Christ as being that mode of life which came into being under his historical impact, we are likely to think first of Christian love as that which the Christian would offer as the distinctive fruit of Christianity. This would invite us to base the claim for the finality of Jesus Christ on the claim that Christian love transcends all other forms of love and cannot itself be surpassed. The preceding chapter points toward this kind of argumentation, and it has its value and importance.

Nevertheless, this kind of argument is exceedingly circular and hence relativistic. The Christian's ideal of love is formed by Jesus Christ, and measured by this ideal, most other ideals seem inadequate. But there are many who doubt the possibility of actualizing this kind of love and point to the self-deceit so often involved on the part of those who claim to do so. There are many also who hold that other ideals of love are intrinsically more noble and beautiful. There are still others who see other characteristics such as justice, self-fulfillment, or truthfulness as of greater worth than love. What is supremely valued is a function of the perspective from which it is valued. What the Christian supremely values is, in truth, supremely valuable only if there is something final about the perspective from which he values it. Hence, the question of valuation is finally directed to these perspectives or structures of existence.

Furthermore, even when the Christian ideal of love is taken as normative, it is impossible to say that Christian love is " higher " than Buddhist love. The Christian himself can conceive no ideal of love higher than that of the Boddhisattva who renounces his own final blessedness for the sake of the world. Viewed simply in itself, there is little to distinguish Buddhist compassion from Christian love. The difference between them is a function of the different structures of existence in which they are found. Buddhist love differs from Christian love in that the Buddhist lover is not a self and, consequently, makes no distinction between lover and beloved, whereas Christian love is that of a self for other selves. Evaluation as between these cannot be on the basis that one or another structure of existence leads to a nobler form of love. Rather, these structures of existence themselves must be evaluated. If the claim that Jesus Christ is final is to be vindicated in terms of his work, then the structure of existence brought into being by him must be shown to be final in some humanly decisive way.

Christian existence has been presented as a unity. But just as there are many modes of existence in which Buddhist, Homeric, Socratic, and prophetic existence have been embodied, so also there have been many modes of existence in which Christian existence has been embodied. Contemporary Christian existence is far removed from that of the Middle Ages, and both are far removed from that of the primitive church. Further, in the primitive church, in the Middle Ages, and today, there is great diversity of modes of Christian existence. In addition, especially in the modern world, there are many who do not call themselves Christians who participate in Christian existence, and, of course, there have always been many who have called themselves Christians who have not participated in it. The claim for the finality of Christian existence is not a claim that any mode of its embodiment now or in the past is final.

Christian existence is spiritual existence fulfilled in love. Since the claim of the finality of Christ has been translated into the claim of the finality of that structure of existence he brought into being, our systematic attention must now be turned to the relation of spiritual existence to other structures of existence. Since not only Christianity but also every other structure of existence is distinctive, this comparison should ultimately entail an individual discussion of the relation of spiritual existence to every other structure of existence. However, this is impractical. Instead, we will consider the Christian claim under three heads. First, in what sense is spiritual existence final within that historical development in which it emerged and came into dominance? Second, in what sense is spiritual existence final with respect to Socratic existence? Third, in what sense is spiritual existence final with respect to Buddhist existence?

Spiritual existence developed out of personal existence (the structure of prophetic existence), which in turn had arisen out of preaxial structures of existence. The questions that demand consideration in claiming finality within this development are the relation of spiritual to personal existence and the possibility of transcending spiritual existence. In limiting serious consideration to these two questions, the superiority of axial existence in general to preaxial existence in general is assumed. Such an assumption would be impossible if superiority were understood in moral terms, even if the standards of morality employed were those given to the Christian. Such preaxial people as the Hopi appear to have achieved a general level of morality in their communities seldom equalled in Christian civilizations. Equally, the superiority of the axial over the preaxial cannot be understood in psychological terms. On the whole, there is probably less emotional illness among more primitive people. Most individuals in simpler societies are better adjusted to those societies and to their roles within them. Maturity, as defined within the culture, is more easily and more widely attained in preaxial communities than in axial ones. Nevertheless, the movement toward rationality, individuality, and freedom is of such attractive force and leads to so great an expansion of power over self and world as to be virtually irreversible.

Of all the questions to be dealt with in this chapter, that of the relation of spiritual to personal existence has been most fully treated in earlier chapters. Spiritual existence was presented as a further development within and of personal existence. The emergence of a center of existence transcending reason and passion, and responsible for decision and action, constituted the unique structure of personal existence. In spiritual existence, this center remained as the will, but it was objectified as one element within the whole psyche and was thereby transcended by a new center that took responsibility also for the will. In this way, spiritual existence took another step along the line away from preaxial existence, incorporating and preserving personal existence in a more inclusive synthesis.

This claim that in spiritual existence personal existence was fulfilled and transformed arises directly out of the descriptions offered in previous chapters, and so far it supports the Christian claim for the finality of Jesus Christ. Yet the continued existence of Judaism is a standing challenge to it. Paul already wrestled with the implicit refutation of his message present in Israel's rejection of Jesus, and for us, too, this constitutes no less acute a theological problem. If indeed Christian existence offers to the Jew the fulfillment through transformation of his own existence, how can it be that millions of Jews have lived among Christians for nineteen centuries, unshaken in the conviction that Christianity represents a distortion of Israel's faith rather than its fulfillment?

An adequate discussion of this topic is out of the question here. However, three points can be mentioned. First, during most of Christian history the church has had its greatest numerical success among preaxial peoples. This is readily understandable. The masses of people in the Hellenistic world, although profoundly affected by the axial revolution, remained primarily in the stage of preaxial civilization. Their world was still essentially mythical. The rapid assimilation of these people meant that the life, worship, and thought of the church were colored by preaxial, mythical elements. The situation was not improved by the vast influx of pagans following the Constantinian establishment of the church or by the mass conversions of the Germanic peoples. The church existed through these centuries as an unstable mixture of preaxial and Christian elements, while Judaism retained, to a far greater degree, the purity of its axial existence. Although *we* may judge that the essential reality which the church always recognized as its norm offered to the Jew a possibility unrealized in his mode of axial existence, we must recognize that he had much justification in seeing Christianity as a corruption of a truth preserved more purely in Judaism.

Second, the treatment of Jews by Christians has consistently, scandalously, and notoriously confronted the Jew with the most unchristian embodiments of spiritual existence. One would like to see the recent and most terrible abominations as simply the product of Hitler's paganism, but this is impossible. Hitler's extermination of millions of Jews is only the climax of a long series of pogroms in which the church has all too often been the chief instigator. One cannot read European history through Jewish eyes without the profoundest shame and a powerful impulse to dissociate oneself forever from the name Christian. Small wonder that the Jew has regarded his own tradition and life as superior.

Third, the classical and official formulations of Christian belief constitute an intellectual obstacle of no mean proportions. The doctrine of Jesus' " deity," however it may be explained by sophisticated theologians, necessarily affronts Jews and appears as a repudiation rather than a fulfillment of their understanding of God.

If the failure of Judaism to perceive in Christian existence its own transcendence and fulfillment is due to such causes as these, then we may look to the future with interest and hope. Now in the national state of Israel, the Jews can reflect on the essence of their own tradition and of Christianity free from the unchristian pressures of a supposedly Christian majority. In these circumstances, they may come to a quite new appraisal of Jesus and of the existence brought into being by him. Also, if the acceptance of the finality of Jesus is dissociated from the acceptance of particular dogmas about him, the obstacles to a full appropriation of Jesus and of spiritual existence would be still further diminished. We should not expect a mass conversion of Jews to Christian churches, but rather an inner transformation of Judaism itself. Perhaps in this way Paul's prophecy will find its fulfillment.

To a great extent this inner transformation has already occurred at the level of the individual. Partly by the subtle influence of a partly Christian civilization and partly by processes of inner development analogous to that in which Christianity itself arose, Western Jews, at least, have already to a large extent entered into spiritual existence. Nevertheless, thus far the transformation of those beliefs and practices which constitute Judaism as a religion has been seriously inhibited by the rejection of Jesus.

If spiritual existence fulfilled and transcended personal existence, we must now ask whether it, in its turn, has been or will be fulfilled and transcended by some other structure of existence. The claim of the finality of spiritual existence implies that no such further development has occurred or is to be expected. Yet such a claim, unless it is carefully restricted, implies both a prescience we do not have and a contradiction of Christian hope. Certainly, we do not wish to say that nothing better is possible than the existence we now know! All Christian images of resurrection and of new life beyond the grave point to something qualitatively new and other. In Jesus himself we see actualized a possibility in crucial respects quite beyond that which we now find realized in ourselves.[24]

In the light of all this, what can it mean to say that spiritual existence is unsurpassable? To explain this we must distinguish two modes of analyzing existence. One mode is that primarily employed in this book in which attention has been focused on the intrapsychic structure, and especially on the center from which the occasion of human experience is organized and unified. The other mode attends to the relations of one occasion of experience with other realities, that is, the ways in which other occasions of experience enter into and give content to a new occasion. In this relational mode, distinctions would be made according to the distinctive roles played by one's own past, one's body, other persons, and God. These two modes of analysis cannot be entirely separated, and this latter mode has played some role in this book, for example, in the analysis of personal individuality through time. However, most of the questions raised by this mode of analysis have been neglected, and in particular the way in which God is present to and in occasions of experience has been omitted from the discussion. Precisely the relationship to God is the decisive category for understanding the distinctiveness of Jesus' own existence or " person " as well as the possibilities of a new reality in the future. In this mode, we can hope for something quite different from anything we now know.

But in the former mode, where intrapsychic structures of existence are in view, spiritual existence cannot be transcended. We have seen how in personal existence a psychic center arose transcending reason and emotion, and how in spiritual existence a new center emerged transcending also that of personal existence, which is now preserved as will. One might suppose that we could then, in a similar way, posit a transcendence of spirit, and so on indefinitely. But this is not the case. Spirit is defined as self-transcending self. It is the nature of spirit to transcend itself in the sense of objectifying itself and assum-

---

[24] The omission from this book of explicit discussion of the structure of Jesus' existence leaves this statement unexplained and unsupported. I hope to treat this subject in a later book.

ing responsibility for itself. Hence, this indefinite transcendence of spirit is also and already spirit. In *this* direction, there is no possibility of further development, only of refinement and increasing understanding of the reality already given.

In terms of the relational categories that have been omitted from this book, this limited statement of the unsurpassability of spiritual existence can be combined with a much stronger claim for the finality of Jesus Christ. The new possibilities for interrelationship among men, and especially of relationship with God, for which we may hope, are already foreshadowed and embodied in him. To move forward across new thresholds will not require some new impulse — only the fuller realization of what has already been given to us in him.

The fulfillment and transcendence by spiritual existence of personal existence, and the unsurpassability of spiritual existence in that line of development in which it arose, go far toward explaining the Christian judgment of the finality of the historical work of Jesus Christ. But the claim goes farther than that. It implies that spiritual existence is related to other structures of axial existence in a similar way. That would mean that spiritual existence is able to fulfill and transcend these other structures of existence as well. This claim will be examined in relation to Socratic and to Buddhist existence.

At first glance, the historical evidence for the Christian claim in relation to Greek existence appears impressive.[25] The great original success of Christianity was among persons who were heirs of Greek civilization. Furthermore, on the whole, the Greeks carried with them into their new Christian faith a continuing positive appreciation of their Greek heritage. They experienced Christianity as its consummation as well as its correction.

Against this rather obvious reading of history, two important objections can be raised, and some indication must be given as to how they can be countered. First, it is possible to view the Christianity of the Hellenistic world as more fundamentally a product of that world than a result of the impact of the Jewish Jesus. In this case, the vic-

---

[25] Although there are a few differences, the following three paragraphs are substantially identical with my material on pp. 133–134 of *The Finality of Christ,* ed. by Dow Kirkpatrick. Copyright © 1966 by Abingdon Press.

tory of Christianity is simply another step in the evolution or devolution of the religious life of Greek civilization. According to this view, the Christianization of the Hellenistic civilization represents an absorption of Judeo-Christian elements into that civilization, but not a transformation or completion by a fundamentally new element introduced from without. My response to this is that despite the immense influence of Hellenistic culture on Christianity, the fundamental institutional, liturgical, and ethical patterns that won out in the struggle within the church are better understood in terms of their Hebraic background than in terms of their Hellenistic background. More important, the canonization of the Old and New Testaments represented the victory of the Hebraic side of the struggle and ensured that, progressively, its peculiar thrust would play a larger rather than a smaller role in the general self-understanding of Christendom.

Second, one may well argue against my view, that although the Hebraic development as consummated in Jesus won out over the decadent Hellenism of the first and second centuries, this tells us nothing of its relationship to the healthy Hellenism of the axial period. From this point of view, it may be claimed that the mentality embodied in the great philosophers is more comprehensively adequate and offers a more final resting place for the human mind than anything that has come out of Israel.

In our day, when the university and the psychological clinic seem to be dividing between them the historic functions of the church, this claim must be given the most serious consideration. Does not Christianity as much as any position live or die according to the validity of its truth claims? Must not these truth claims, like all other truth claims, be judged at the court of reason? Does not every attempt to escape this court of last appeal depend on ideas of authority or revelation or intuition, which can function responsibly only when they in turn are rationally tested? Is it not exceedingly dangerous to claim that some decisions or some areas of life are or should be free from the control of reason? Does not the appeal to reason bring men closer together, whereas every other appeal — to emotion or to willful decision — drive them apart? Is not unity in our day a matter of extreme importance?

My own answer to all these questions is affirmative. Insofar as this affirmative answer constitutes the adoption of the Socratic standpoint, I plead guilty to being a Socratic. If being a Christian means the acceptance on " faith " of beliefs that have not been subjected to critical reflection, then it is Christianity which can and should be subsumed within a Socratic synthesis. That would mean that the content of Christian belief would be critically evaluated and much of it accepted from a standpoint which lay outside of it, the standpoint of reason. Just this was the program of much nineteenth-century idealism, which was thereby in intention Socratic.

The Christian counterclaim, that it is in the last analysis Christianity which absorbs the Socratic achievement, depends on the view that although beliefs are important, the issue is finally at a still deeper level. In this book, it is formulated in terms of the structures of existence. The claim is that spiritual existence can fulfill and transform Socratic existence in a way in which Socratic existence cannot fulfill and transform itself or Christian existence. The basis of this claim can first be shown in the comparison of the two structures of existence. Socratic man identifies himself with his reason, which he recognizes as one element within his psyche. Spiritual existence is constituted by the emergence of an " I " that transcends reason and passion and will as well as itself. To incorporate such an " I " is impossible without ceasing to identify oneself with one's reason, whereas the reason of Socratic man can be incorporated into spiritual existence.

The claim that spiritual existence fulfills and transcends Socratic existence, however, must mean more than that Socratic reason *can* be incorporated into Christian existence. It must mean also that there is something about Socratic existence which calls for this expansion into a larger whole with a changed center.

Greek existence came into being through an act of aesthetic distancing of nature and the gods, which freed the Greek to become aware of the formal properties of the world. Reason came into importance in dealing with these forms, and even when it was turned upon itself and upon the soul as a whole, it had no other kind of categories by which to think than those which were achieved by this psychic act of distancing. Primitive Christianity did not of itself provide the requisite categories, but the self-transcending self of Christian existence knew itself and the psyche as something other than the sensuously experienced world. When it absorbed, as in Augustine, the Socratic passion for knowledge, it was able to achieve a language and a quality of self-knowledge inaccessible within Socratic existence itself.

A similar limitation can be seen in Socrates' immensely impressive ethical achievement. Because of the essential character of Socratic existence, the identification of the self with active reason, Socrates could not attribute to the self a responsibility for the evil which a man enacted. Since the self *is* reason, it is necessarily good. If evil transpires, this can only mean that the self is overpowered by an alien force, and reason cannot be responsible for its own defeat. Socrates' own life and thought point to an inchoate awareness of a responsibility that could not be expressed in these terms, but just here lay a threshold that could only be crossed by some structural change. This structural change was offered by Christianity, which in this way also fulfilled the fundamental direction of the Socratic development.

With respect to the thesis that spiritual existence is the fulfillment and transcendence of Socratic existence, a qualification is necessary. The incorporation of Socratic reason within Christianity introduced an element that holds also the possibility of the destruction of spiritual existence. This is not because the prizing of reason or its high development as such threatens the self-transcending self of spiritual existence. But insofar as the perpetuation of this self-transcending self depends on beliefs of any sort, it is vulnerable. The history of Christian theology can be read as the attempt to employ and develop reason, on the one hand, and so to direct and restrict it, on the other, as to preserve the possibility of Christian existence. Such restrictions have always been wrong, and today are quite out of the question. The possibility that the use of reason by spiritual man will destroy the beliefs with which Christian existence is most closely associated and on which it seems ultimately to depend must be accepted. Where this occurs, however, there is no simple return to Socratic existence. The self-knowledge gleaned during the Christian era has left too large a legacy to allow for this. Partly for this reason, the great traditions of

India offer themselves to the Western mind as powerfully attractive alternatives to the structures of existence that arose in Israel and Greece.

Both historically and systematically, the relation of spiritual existence to Indian existence is radically different from its relation to either personal or Socratic existence. In the case of both personal and Socratic existence, consciousness, selfhood, and the power of the soul to transcend and to act upon its world were prized. Spiritual existence carried farther in the same direction a development already affirmed and far advanced. Thus we can speak of fulfillment as well as transcendence or transformation of existing structures. But the Indian sages of the axial period had opposed this whole line of psychic development. To them it was essential either to establish the self beyond the differentiated world, which included the flow of psychic experience, or to annihilate selfhood altogether. Spiritual existence is not the fulfillment of this effort. Nor can the Christian recognize in extinction of his self-transcending selfhood the fulfillment of his existence. Finally, it is impossible to conceive a third structure in which both spiritual selfhood and the extinction of self could be subsumed in some higher synthesis. Buddhism, as the culminating achievement of India, lies side by side with Christianity as an alternative mode of human realization. It stands as the ultimate challenge and limit to the Christian claim to finality.

Nevertheless, there are judgments that can be made between the two. These are not systematic judgments and, from the point of view of the Buddhist for whom the events of history are meaningless, they are without importance. But from the point of view of one who lives in history and by his understanding of history, the judgments must be made. These are judgments about the relative capacity of Buddhist and spiritual existence to survive in the ever smaller world in which we live. These judgments do not unambiguously favor either Buddhism or Christianity.

At the level of belief, Buddhism today has much advantage. Socratic reason, in its modern scientific form, has rendered the Buddhist doctrines of no-self and no-God more plausible to many modern men than opposed Christian convictions. Whereas Christianity is in these crucial respects in a crisis of belief, Buddhism in its axial form feels secure. If present trends continue unabated, Christian belief must disappear, and if, as I believe, spiritual existence cannot indefinitely survive the loss of such beliefs, spiritual existence also is doomed. In that case, we should be grateful that the world is offered the Buddhist alternative to Western nihilism.

However, I am not myself persuaded of the inevitability of this outcome. The assumption that underlies and comes to expression in this book is that although the Buddhist goal of annihilating selfhood is a possible one, the selfhood that the Buddhist annihilates is also real and quite capable of rich development. If we are confronted with the two possibilities of being self-transcending selves or overcoming selfhood, then we cannot suppose that scientific knowledge decisively opposes the conception of selfhood. Similarly, it is my conviction that our scientific knowledge of the world can best be fitted with our human self-awareness and with the witness of aesthetic and religious experience in a comprehensive synthesis that points to the reality of God. In this conviction, I am heavily indebted to Whitehead, and I have written about the understanding of God that is involved in *A Christian Natural Theology*. Thus my own beliefs allow for and support spiritual existence, and I could not hold these beliefs if I did not find them to have great persuasive power. If they or similar beliefs do have such power, then spiritual existence is not doomed to extinction. The present advantage of Buddhism at the level of beliefs may be temporary.

The second element in a judgment of survival power is more favorable to spiritual existence. It is now inevitable that the technological results of modern science will spread throughout the world. This spread adds greatly to the prestige of science itself, and this, too, is certain to become a universal factor. But modern science is essentially Western, and that means that the context for its rise and development was the incorporation of Socratic reason into Christian existence. The history of science is intertwined with a philosophy that even more clearly witnesses to this context. Entry into the modern world cannot be simply the acceptance of technology but must also involve acceptance of aspects of that structure of existence which has nurtured it. The modernization all Eastern nations want is inescapably also Westernization, and Westernization involves, to some degree, the emergence of the responsible " I."

The question mark that is placed beside Christianity has to do with its capacity to survive the consequences of autonomous reason. The question mark that is placed beside Buddhism has to do with its capacity to survive in a world in which the cultural forces will work so strongly to produce the personal or spiritual selfhood which it negates. The answer to this question is objectively no clearer than the other. Yet I must record my judgment that in a world destined to Westernization in all outward ways, the Westernization of the soul is almost inevitable.

It may be, of course, that this Westernization will occur in radically post-Christian terms. Perhaps the structure of spiritual existence is already being superseded among us by other structures to which the sense of the " loss of self " witnesses, but which do not seem to lead to the serenity of Buddhist selflessness. Seidenberg paints a depressing picture of that " posthistoric man," [26] into which he says we are evolving. But I am not convinced that this must be. We have far from exhausted the possibilities of self-transcending selfhood, and in our infinitely complex society, there are forces at work extending and enriching this selfhood as well as forces which are undermining it or seeking escape from it. The outcome is unsettled. This situation in which the destiny of man hangs in the balance is the ultimate call for new modes of Christian existence.

[26] Roderick Seidenberg, *Posthistoric Man* (Beacon Press, Inc., 1957). The original edition was published in 1950 by the University of North Carolina Press.

Appendix

GNOSTICISM

THIS BOOK has at no point claimed completeness. Not only are the stages of preaxial development treated only formally and the axial cultures of China and Persia wholly omitted, but also developments in Greece and Palestine have been dealt with schematically in such a way as to ignore other modes of existence which took shape within them. Hence, no special apology is appropriate for the omission of one or another particular movement.

However, the avowed principle of selection and emphasis has been interest in Christian existence, and this has been presented quite simply as an outgrowth of prophetic existence. I do not apologize for this arrangement of the material, and I hope that in part the presentation in terms of structures of existence lends justification to this embattled view. Nevertheless, the view *is* an embattled one. The close affinities of Christianity to contemporary Hellenistic alternatives compel us to consider the extent to which it should be understood against this background instead of that of the earlier Hebrew prophetism and its peculiar consequences in Israel. Even the term " spiritual existence " points directly to such affinities with Hellenism.

Although the Hellenistic alternatives to Christianity are highly varied, they tend to be distinguishable from Socratic existence by traits which in their full-blown form constitute Gnosticism. Gnosticism is here understood as that movement of the later Hellenistic world which sought salvation from the whole cosmos regarded as, in principle, an alien and evil power. It is to be distinguished, thereby, both from Socratic and from prophetic existence. To grasp what is entailed in this definition, it must be understood that the cosmos includes the human body and even the human soul as a whole.

I am in no position to enter into the historical debate as to the relative importance of the several sources of Gnosticism, but I must attempt to place it in reference to the schematism of this book. In confronting this task, one is faced first by the exceedingly extensive use of mythical material by the Gnostics. In spite of this, Gnosticism must be recognized as an axial phenomenon. That is, it reflects the shift of the seat of existence to consciousness and the consequent objectification of the mythical products of the unconscious. However, in this case, unlike those of Socratic and prophetic existence, men experienced themselves as thrust out of preaxial existence by partly unwelcome forces, concretely the cultural imperialism of the Hellenistic empires, which drew men toward Socratic existence.

In its own origins, Socratic existence presupposed the prior victory of Homeric existence over the mythical powers, but in its spread through Syria, Egypt, and Mesopotamia, this precondition did not obtain. Cultural intermixture plus Persian influence had brought these regions to the brink of axial existence, and some universalization and systematization of myth preceded Hellenization, providing the possibility for taking the myths seriously also from the Hellenic point of view. In this situation, alongside the possibility of rejecting the mythical lay the other possibility of seeking in it meanings intelligible to the rational consciousness, and structuring and elaborating the mythical material so as to give expression to these meanings. Thus the form of Gnostic self-expression can be understood as a consequence of the direct impact of Socratic existence on highly civilized peoples prepared for the axial revolution, but not yet freed from the dominant power of the mythical.

More important than the mythological form of Gnostic expression, however, was the content expressed. This can be interpreted in the same way. From the beginning of civilization, men experienced an inner estrangement between their rational consciousness and the psyche as a whole. This estrangement gained expression in myth and was thereby contained. The shift of the seat of existence to the rational consciousness, however, created an alienation of the self from the unconscious psychic life as a whole. Thus the sense of alienation was an inevitable element in all axial existence.

Where the transition from preaxial to axial existence occurred not by internal cultural development but by the impact of a foreign proselytizing culture, the sense of alienation was greatly intensified. The Socratic world into which Egyptian or Syrian man was called by Hellenization was indeed an alien and resented world. From this world there was no return to simply mythical existence, but myths and other ancient traditions could yet be made to yield an expression of the hostility felt toward it. The sense of alienation both from the unconscious and from the world of Socratic reason created a consciousness of self or spirit as something wholly other to all the rest of the psychic life.

According to this theory, Gnosticism was primarily the product of the less completely Hellenized peoples of the Hellenistic world for whom, nevertheless, Hellenization was the agency by which they were carried across the axial threshold. Among those who experienced the impact of Hellenization in this way were also those inhabitants of Greece and Israel who had earlier participated, but fragmentarily, in the dominant cultures of these peoples. To appraise the total role of Gnosticism, however, it is important to see that the sense of alienation which received such pure expression in Gnosticism played its independent part also in the dominant axial cultures of Greece and Palestine, where it was initially contained as a subdominant element in a larger synthesis. Only in this way can we understand both the parallel developments in these cultures and the readiness with which fusion sometimes occurred.

In Greece, Homeric men undertook to domesticate the alien powers within an aesthetically ordered world. In Israel, prophetic man attempted a moral ordering of the whole of life in response to his apprehension of the divine will. Neither attempt was entirely successful. Within both traditions the sense of alien and even hostile powers made itself felt. In Greece, this was in terms of an always limiting and sometimes oppressive fate and of the struggle to master the Dionysian spirit. In Israel, the pull toward disobedience required a doctrine of a tempter, and the injustices of life confronted man with an insoluble problem of evil. This meant in both Greece and Israel that man could not be entirely at home in the world, that there existed between himself and his world an element of tension. Nevertheless, for Homeric man the understanding of the world as cosmos, as intelligible order, remained fundamental, and for prophetic man the tempter was radically subordinated to the Creator-Lawgiver.

The flowering and transformation of Greek culture in Socrates continued the dominance of the sense of order but heightened the implicit tension. Man identified himself with one factor within reflective consciousness. This factor was still perceived as in harmony with the cosmos as a whole, but this harmony with ultimate cosmic reality must be contrasted with its frequent opposition to such inferior aspects of the cosmos as the physical and the emotional life of the soul. In Stoicism, the contradiction between reason and all else in the body and soul was carried to an extreme point, and although reason still claimed kinship with nature and cosmos, most of what *we* regard as "natural" was ruthlessly suppressed.

Similarly, in some forms of Jewish apocalypticism, the tension between the felt injustice of history and faith in the God who was Creator and Lord of history reached an extreme pitch. All that was factually given to man in this life was dissociated from the work of the Creator-God, except as signs and portents of a total transformation to come in which faith would at last be vindicated.

From one point of view, it was not a great step from the Stoic hostility toward the irrational to Gnostic condemnation of the world as a whole. Yet it was just that kind of step which I have called the crossing of a threshold. It was the accentuation of one element in a given synthesis to that point at which the old synthesis collapsed and a new one was formed around a new center. When this step was taken, the aesthetic and rational order fundamental to Greek existence was abandoned. Hence, the center of existence could no longer be reason. Instead, it had to be identified with "spirit"! At this point, a movement growing out of the inner development of Greek existence could be receptive to and even merge with the Gnosticism that had essentially bypassed this development.

The relation of Jewish apocalypticism to Gnosticism was similar, although not identical. Despite the world-denying emphasis of apocalypticism, Jewish apocalypticism never rejected the Torah. Hence, the movement from apocalypticism to the Gnostic rejection of law was more abrupt than that from Stoicism. The choice between Judaism, even in its most apocalyptic forms, and Gnosticism remained clear-cut. It was directly from apocalyptic Judaism that Christianity arose, rather than from Gnosticism. Nevertheless, the significant affinities are also apparent.

It is because of the close parallel with Christian existence, especially in the understanding of selfhood, that it is not possible to omit this brief discussion of Gnosticism from this book. Christian existence has been described as spiritual existence fulfilled in love, and the rise of spiritual existence has been identified with that of Christian existence. Yet we find that, independently of Christianity, "spiritual existence" was the self-definition of the Gnostic as well. Furthermore, the meaning of "spirit" in the two cases was similar. For both it referred to the self or the "I" as the center that transcended all such other elements in the psyche as reason and will. In both cases there was a close correlation between this transcending human spirit and the God who transcended the world.

Nevertheless, there was a profound difference between "spirit" in Gnosticism and in Christianity, such that by the definition of "spiritual existence" in this book, the Gnostic did not participate in it. This difference can be explained in terms of responsibility. The Gnostic as "spirit" transcended all other elements in his psychic life in the sense that he differentiated himself from them and distanced them. He experienced some power in respect to them in the sense that he might either repress them or gratify their several inclinations. But he accepted no responsibility for them. Their evil character was none of his doing, and if they entrapped him or gained mastery over him, that was the work of forces alien to himself.

Similarly, Gnostic "spirit" was *self*-transcendent in the sense that it knew itself as such, but it took no responsibility for itself. It understood itself as a supernatural entity caught or implanted in the natural psyche. In its own being it was simply good. Whatever responsibility the Gnostic may in fact have felt for the state of his "spirit," his self-understanding allowed no explication in such terms, and to a considerable degree the implications of this lack of responsibility for what one's self was was consistently developed in theory and practice.

Whether the Gnostic understanding of the relation of the "spirit" to other elements in the psyche resulted from or was projected onto the understanding of God's relation to the created world, the close correlation and mutual reinforcement is apparent. God transcended the world in the sense that he was outside the world and other than the world. God even had some power with respect to what transpired within the world. Nevertheless, he had no responsibility for the world. It was something wholly alien to him. His only kinship lay with men, insofar as men were " spirits."

Having indicated both the close parallel between Gnostic and Christian existence and also the difference, I can explain why the account of this threshold crossing was omitted from the body of the book. The fundamental reason is that it appears to have been abortive. Gnosticism did succeed in extricating the self from its identification with reason and will, and in this respect it went beyond Socratic and prophetic existence. But it did so in such a way as not to incorporate or fulfill Socratic and prophetic existence but so as to negate them. What would have occurred had Hellenistic man not received in Christianity the possibility of transcending the limits of Socratic and prophetic existence without their negation, one can only conjecture. But in fact the Christian alternative did appear and was victorious.

Even if Gnosticism in its distinction from Christianity is recognized as finally abortive, the critic might argue that the rise of Christian existence as such presupposes Gnosticism. In this case, a chapter on Gnostic existence should be placed between those on prophetic and Christian existence. My reasons for rejecting this should now be clear. The world-rejecting elements in Christianity are adequately explained by Jewish apocalypticism, and this, despite its enmity toward the present world, stopped short of and opposed the dissolution of moral order. Christianity continued and even heightened the apocalyptic sense of estrangement of the self from the given historical situation, but it heightened also the sense of total responsibility for the soul. It acknowledged its kinship with Gnosticism by employing some of its terminology, but it correctly recognized in Gnosticism not its parent but its most dangerous enemy.

INDEX